100 QUESTIONS AND BIBLICAL ANSWERS ON MARRIAGE AND FAMILY RELATIONSHIPS

ALSO AVAILABLE IN FRENCH

ISBN: 9798518451599

By

HE Pastor Dr. Mrs. Cecilia Gbemisola Obisakin

Wife of PICP RCCG Republic of Benin Province 1, Cotonou.

INTRODUCTION

"And we know that all things work together for good to those who love God, to those who are called according to His purpose" Romans 8:28.

All thanks to the Almighty God, the Sovereign of the universe and the God of all nations for the opportunity given me to realize the dream of writing a hundred questions and biblical answers on marriage. This book is for the reading pleasure of every member of the family, most especially the youth as they prepare for marriage. The book was written while under lockdown because of Covid 19 pandemic, in Cotonou, Republic of Benin between May and June 2020.

What is COVID 19? The COVID-19 pandemic, also known as the coronavirus pandemic, is an ongoing pandemic of coronavirus disease 2019, caused by severe acute respiratory syndrome coronavirus 2. The outbreak was first identified in Wuhan, China, in December 2019. The World Health Organization declared the outbreak a Public Health Emergency of International Concern on 30 January 2020, and a pandemic on 11 March. As of 16 June 2020, more than 8 million cases of COVID-19 have been reported in more than 180 countries all over the word with thousands of casualties.

By the special grace of God 1 am a Sanguine – choleric in temperament. I love to have people around me, I enjoy a lot of physical and spiritual activities, 1 am always on the move. To be locked down at home, not being able to go out, to travel, to interact with my women folks and attend church services   for 72 days – precisely from the Family Worship Service of Sunday March 22nd to the Bible study – Digging Deep of Tuesday May 19th, 2020 became a serious challenge to me, here in Cotonou, Benin Republic.

I was really getting tired and sick of the boredom, lack of movement and   inactivity. To go to the Gym for physical exercises was forbidden, taking a walk outside the house was dangerous, the use of face mask was a big burden, I wasn't just comfortable with it. When you think of the constant washing of hands with soap and water, sanitizing, distancing an inability to hug or shake hands with people, you don't even want to go out. It was a hard time.

However, despite all the consequences of Covid 19, I had a good time studying the book of Psalms and Proverbs, reading a chapter of Proverbs and two or three chapters of the book of Psalms every day. They were the tonic to my joints and bones that kept me up and doing, and I am really blessed. One day, as I was digging deep into my Bible in the early hours, first week of May – (I like to study my Bible   with "DAKE'S ANNOTATED REFERENCE BIBLE" By Finis Jennings Dake, Large Print Edition April 2005)   the Holy Spirit reminded me of the one hundred questions and biblical answers that I had wanted to write.

To the glory of God here is the book. I was to celebrate my 60th birthday on August 2nd (I was born on July 27th 1960) at the RCCG Camp in Lagos, but I had to postpone it to December 5th, 2020 due to the same Covid 19 lockdown. Without the Covid 19 plague, this book may not have been written this year. Out of what seems to be a very difficult period of my life God helped me through the Lord

Jesus Christ, and with the help of the Holy Spirit to bring out this book. Let somebody shout Alleluia!

I am so glad you are going to read this book. God bless you more abundantly as you read and apply the knowledge shared on marriage and marital relationships in the book. The questions were generated from real life experiences, the concerns, interrogations from and discussion with Counselees. As an international marriage counselor of over thirty years, my counselees cut across different nations, race, status and age, but we offer only biblical advice to them in accordance with the Word of God.

Take time to read this book and pass it on to others. This book may be used as a wedding gifts for newlyweds. God will surely use it to encourage, inform, reform, correct and establish innumerous members of the family in the name of Jesus. Amen.

DEDICATION

This book is fondly dedicated to my own dear husband of almost four decades now!

His Excellency, Pastor, Lawrence Olufemi Obisakin (Ph.D.)

For the golden opportunity to be married to a Child of God, who became a Man of God,

An Ambassador of Nigeria extra-ordinary and Plenipotentiary,

 A quintessential diplomat, an Ambassador for Christ, and A great husband.

You made me travel all over the world, acquiring life - impacting knowledge and become serviceable to God and Mankind. I appreciate all you have done to make me all what I have become under your love, care, encouragement and support.

I thank God for your life, and I am grateful to you for all.

I love you, and I will continue to do so, till eternity with Christ. Amen.

Forever Yours,

Cecilia Gbemisola Obisakin.

TABLE OF CONTENTS

PAGE

J. CONFLICT MANAGEMENT IN THE FAMILY

AND RELATIONSHIP WITH IN-LAWS

FAMILY CRISIS AND HOW TO HANDLE THEM

DEATH – THE END OF MARRIAGE

GENERAL QUESTIONS ON MARRIAGE

1. WHAT IS MARRIAGE?

Marriage is the union of a single man and a single woman in the Lord. Marriage is the official beginning of the family, it is the social platform from which the family is launched. Marriage is a lifelong covenant of companionship between a man and a woman that has been established under God and His people.

Other definitions - "Marriage is an exclusive, heterosexual covenant between one man and one woman, ordained and seal by God, preceded by a public leaving of parents, consummated in sexual union, issuing in a permanent mutually supportive partnership, and normally crowned by the gift of children" – John R. W. Scott.

"Marriage is the intimate, exclusive, indissoluble communion of life and love entered by man and woman at the design of the Creator for the purpose of their own good and for procreation and education of children" – Saint Pope John Paul II 1978 -2005.

"Then the Lord God said, "It is not good that the man should be alone; I will make him a helper fit for him." Therefore a man shall leave his father and his mother and hold fast to his wife, and they shall become one flesh." Genesis 2: 18, 24.

2. WHOSE IDEA IS MARRIAGE? HOW IS MARRIAGE DIVINE?

Marriage is no man's idea, it is God's idea. Marriage is divine because God is the founder and sustainer of the marriage institution. Marriage is borne out of the love of God for mankind, and so that man may fulfill the plan and purpose of God in life.

18 Then the Lord God said, "It is not good that the man should be alone; I will make him a helper fit for him." 21 So the Lord God caused a deep sleep to fall upon the man, and while he slept took one of his ribs and closed up its place with flesh. 22 And the rib that the Lord God had taken from the man he made into a woman and brought her to the man. 23 Then the man said, "This at last is bone of my bones and flesh of my flesh; she shall be called Woman, because she was taken out of Man." Genesis 2: 18, 21-23.

3.   WHY DID GOD ORDAIN MARRIAGE?

When the purpose of a course is unknown, abuse is inevitable. Many people have many reasons for getting married but according to the Bible, God instituted marriage for these purposes:-

To solve the problem of loneliness – Gen. 2:18

To make man have a suitable helper – Gen. 2:18

To avoid fornication, to provide room for legitimate sexual relationship between a husband and wife - "Nevertheless, to avoid fornication, let every man have his own wife, and let every woman have her own husband". 1 Corinthians 7:2

For the progeny of human kind, for childbearing and child raising – "So God created man in his own image, in the image of God created he him; male and female created he them. 28 And God blessed them, and God said unto them, be fruitful, and multiply, and replenish the earth, and subdue it..." Genesis 1:27-28

To typify, illustrate and reflect the sacrificial love of Christ for the church. Agape – the unconditional love of God is best demonstrated in marriage. "Husbands, love your wives, even as Christ also loved the church, and gave himself for it" So husbands ought also to love their own wives as their own bodies. He who loves his own wife loves himself

Ephesians 5:25, 28.

4. WHY IS THE CHRISTIAN MARRIAGE SO SPECIAL?

The Christian or Biblical marriage is marriage according to the will of God as illustrated in the Bible. It is different from the Legal or court marriage or the traditional marriage rites done according to the culture and practices of people – Genesis 2: 18 -25. It is unique because:-

It is the union of a Christian man and a Christian woman in the Lord

No room for bestiality, polygamy, polyandry, homosexuality and lesbianism in biblical Christianity

There is no dating and no cohabitation before wedding

No sexual intercourse before wedding

They are not getting married because the woman is pregnant

The foundation of the relationship is the love of God in Christ – not money, beauty, sex, position, power or connection

Hearts are united in Agape – the unconditional love of God; it is the ruling love genuinely manifesting in Phileo, Eros and Storge

It is patterned after the love of Christ for the church, husband loves the wife as Christ loves the church and gave His life for it, wife submits unto the husband as unto the Lord

Childlessness, sickness, poverty or lack are no grounds for divorce

The relationship is forever – till death do part marriage partners!

No separation, No divorce! No second marriage.

IS IT COMPULSORY FOR EVERYONE TO MARRY? WOULD EVERYONE EVER GET MARRIED?

It is not compulsory for anyone to marry, as a matter of fact not every single person would be married for one reason or the other.

However, from the scriptures we can see that we are created for marriage "So God created man in his own image, in the image of God created he him; male and female created he them Genesis 2:27.

God did not create us male and female for nothing. It is neither good for man nor woman to be alone, two heads will always be better than one –

Two are better than one, because they have a good return for their labor: If either of them falls down, one can help the other up. But pity anyone who falls and has no one to help them up. Also, if two lie down together, they will keep warm. But how can one keep warm alone? Ecclesiastes 4:9-11.

As the highest animals created by God humans are social beings, our sexuality crave for relationship, no man or woman is an island, we need each other to enjoy life and to fulfill our purposes in life. That is why the family is the nucleus of every human society.

There are some people who have vowed never to be married because of religious commitment as in the Catholic Church – Reverend fathers and sisters. Some due to some diseases or hormone disorder may not be able to marry. Some men cannot marry because they have been born eunuchs and some men allowed themselves to be made eunuchs. Eunuchs are not naturally fit for marriage because they cannot relate sexually with women.

For there are some eunuchs, which were so born from their mother's womb: and there are some eunuchs, which were made eunuchs of men: and there be eunuchs, which have made themselves eunuchs for the kingdom of heaven's sake. He that is able to receive it, let him receive it Matthew 19:12.

5.   WHAT DO I STAND TO LOSE IF I CHOOSE TO REMAIN SINGLE?

It is written - "I can do all things through Christ which strengthens me." Phil. 4:13. "For with God nothing shall be impossible" Luke 1:37.

If you like to remain single, it is your own choice, you can be by the grace of God whatever you want to be. Societies nowadays are full of singles never married people, sometimes ago this was not normal. You may have your reason(s) for wanting to remain single. If you have been jilted or disappointed before or you have entered into many relationships that did not end in marriage as expected, you may think the best way to proof yourself stronger in this situation is to remain single. I would rather advise you to seek counsel - Without counsel purposes are disappointed: but in the multitude of counselors they are established. Prov. 15:22.

If you really want to be single in life you have nothing to lose; spiritually you are in a better position to worship and serve God. You have more time to serve God than the married who are concerned always with their family affairs. "I would like you to be free from concern. An unmarried man is concerned about the Lord's affairs — how he can please the Lord". I Corinthians 7:32.

Unless you are forced by situation beyond your human power, it is advisable for you to go for marriage. As a single, you will not be able to enjoy God's reasons for creating marriage. That is you will be lonely, you will not have a real close intimate helper, you cannot enjoy the mutual pleasure sex gives or have children throughout your life. If you ever do indulge in sex outside marriage, it will be a sin, a willful disobedience to God that attracts grievous consequences.   You may have to battle with boredom, temptations and frustrations associated with being alone. You are also susceptible to selfishness, envy and jealous of the married and may regret your decision to remain single later in life. It is really not good for anyone to be alone, man or woman, that is why God created us male and female.

6.   WHAT ARE THE BENEFITS OF MARRIAGE?

Marriage is divine and God has his reasons for founding this oldest and the greatest human relationship. Read Genesis 2: 18 -25. Genesis 1: 27 -28. In marriage –

You obtain the favor of good and you fulfill the plan and purposes of God for mankind

You are in dominion, you are to be fruitful and multiply

You are not alone, two are always better than one

You have a companion to fellowship with

You have a life partner to relate with sexually

You belong to someone, someone is always physically and emotionally close to you

You impact the world better as father and mother, your children are God's heritage

You are able to demonstrate Agape – the unconditional love of God better in your cordial and committed relationship to your spouse

Two of you will work better for God, you will chase ten thousands for Him

You have a good influence on your society as a godly family, let the beauty of Jesus be seen in you, His wondrous compassion and purity

The world will see your foot prints in your Christian legacy from generation to generation

7.   I AM A CHRISTIAN SISTER- 38 YEARS OLD, NOBODY HAS EVER ASKED FOR MY HAND IN MARRIAGE, WHAT IS GOING ON?

Normally when you are of marriageable age and there is no suitor, it is a cause for concern. I want you to know that you are not the only one in this situation. Singleness is a stage in life and it will come to pass sooner or later if you would trust God, be patient, watchful and prayerful. There hath no temptation taken you but such as is common to man: but God is faithful, who will not suffer you to be tempted above that ye are able; but will with the temptation also make a way to escape, that ye may be able to bear it". . 1 Corinthians 10:13

Do you have any challenge physically? Mentally? Morally? Or socially? If not, what is your educational level? Are you in a position to support a husband? – Do you have any source of income at all? You may be wondering – "Why all these questions?" Nowadays some of these factors affect the choice of a life partner.

Not many men are willing to marry someone that would be a liability. As a helper a wife – to - be should be educated enough to manage home affairs, have some skills or training formally or informally and should be mentally fit to run the race of marriage. It is also possible that a past life of social recklessness and moral depravity will affect final settlement in marriage negatively. As a Christian, God will forgive but there are consequences of ungodliness that may mar the hope of a blissful marriage. Prevention is always better than cure.

Finally, the Bible says our warfare is not carnal but spiritual. Your compulsory state of singleness could be due to spiritual wickedness. Your delay in marriage may be due to demonic coverage, covenant or curses. You may have to go for deliverance, and your victory is sure in the name of Jesus.

"Blotting out the handwriting of ordinances that was against us, which was contrary to us, and took it out of the way, nailing it to his cross; And having spoiled principalities and powers, he made a shew of them openly, triumphing over them in it" Colossians 2:14-15.

8.   MEN ALWAYS USED ME AND DUMPED ME –I HAVE HAD MANY RELATIONSHIPS BUT NONE HAS RESULTED IN MARRIAGE. WHY?

God the founder of marriage has rules and regulations that govern marriage according to His Plan and purposes as written in the Bible. From what you have said, I have a feeling that these relationships have not been according to the will of God. When God is in a relationship there will be no question of being used and dumped.

Used in what sense? I guess you mean you have been sexually involved with men, financially exploited and may be physically and emotionally abused by men. These ought not to have been the case at all. You may be suffering the consequences of dating. Children of God don't go on dating, they are engaged to be married and go into courtship wish should result in marriage. Though not all courtships end in marriage, even among the very few that could not marry for obvious reasons, there are no regrets.

Dating is not biblical, it is a social, worldly affairs and the consequences are usually grievous. "Do not be deceived: God cannot be mocked. Whatever a man sows, he will reap in return. 8 The one who sows to please his flesh, from the flesh will reap destruction; but the one who sows to please the Spirit, from the Spirit will reap eternal life…" Galatians 6: 7-8.

You must stop going into relationship casually. Repent of your ungodly ways. Be truly born again. Marriage is divine, spiritual and it needs a divine, spiritual foundation through Christ. When you are saved, forgiven, sanctified and filled with the Holy Spirit, you will be able to enter marriage in a godly manner through spiritual courtship and not by natural dating.

Now the natural person does not receive the things of the Spirit of God, for they are foolishness to him, and he cannot understand them, because they are spiritually discerned. I Corinthians 2:14.

PREPARATION FOR MARRIAGE

---

9. WHAT IS THE IDEAL AGE FOR MARRIAGE? IS THERE AN AGE LIMIT FOR MARRIAGE?

"To everything there is a season, and a time to every purpose under the heaven: 2 A time to be born, and a time to die; a time to plant, and a time to pluck up that which is planted" Ecclesiastes 3: 1-2.

Of course there is a time to be married too. Human Life is in a circle from the womb – cradle to the grave. Though many factors such as environment, education, job opportunity, experience, security and social stability are bound to affect the time when one gets married, marriage is for the matured men and women. Marriage is not for teenagers. The fact that a boy or girl has reached the age of puberty –18 years and above or adolescence does not mean he or she is ready to marry.

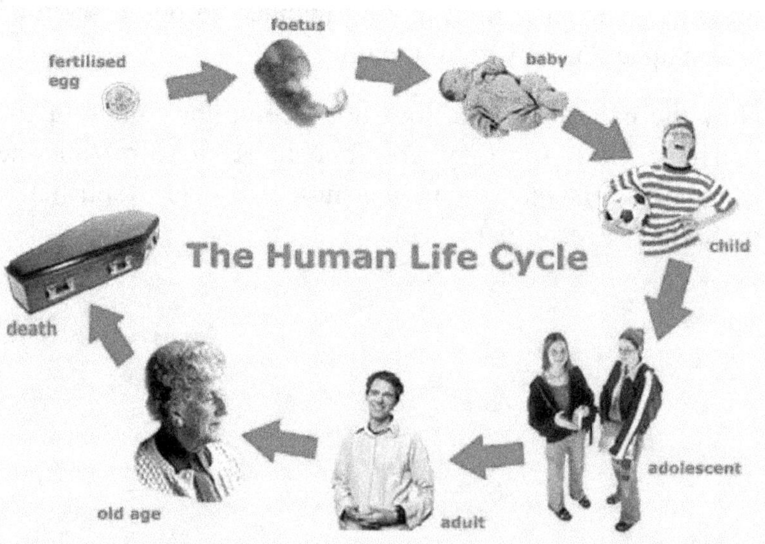

Biologically, the ideal age for marriage for boys is between 25 – 30. It is medically advisable for girls to attain the age of 22 and above before marriage, at this age, the reproductory system is strong enough to go through the rigor of pregnancy, labor and childbirth. The problem of Vesico –Vaginal Fistula (VVF) will be drastically reduced if this instruction is followed. VVF is one of the complications of childbirth that results in continuous involuntary discharge of urine into the vagina among teenage girls who were forced to deliver babies through immature narrow pelvic. In counseling we refer to them as "Baby mothers".

Marriage should take place between late adolescent 22 years and above and before old age – after 30 years and above.

It is still possible for a man and a woman to marry at old age for companionship, or to solve the problem of loneliness of a widow or widower.

Waiting to marry till age of 40 years and above is a kind of selfishness or self-centeredness. The children born at this age may not have proper care and total education because the father would have retired or be on the verge of retirement by the time the financial help of the father is needed for tertiary education.

According to the Bible – Psalm 90:10 –" The days of our lives are seventy years; And if by reason of strength they are eighty years, Yet their boast is only labor and sorrow; For it is soon cut off, and we fly away",

According to the latest world map published in 2019 by the United Nations for life expectancy, life expectancy of the people in West Africa is between 55 -65 years. Life expectancy is a measure of premature death and it shows large differences in health across the world.

If that is the case, marriage should happen between adolescence and adulthood   between 23-30 years of age. Middle age is between 35 – 45 years of age. Adulthood is between 45 -60 and old age if from 60 and above. Marriage of companionship, for fellowship for widows and widowers can take place before old age.

HEAR THIS ABOUT THE CYCLE OF HUMAN LIFE

—

"At 1 year old, success is when you can walk without a support.

At 4 years old, success is when you no longer urinate in your pants.

At 8 years old, success is when you know your way back home from school.

At 12 years old, success is to have friends and to have finished primary school

At 18 years old, success is when you have finished secondary school and you can get a driving license

At 23 years old, success is when you have graduated from a university

At 25 years old, success is when you start earning an income

At 30 years old, success is when you are a family man.

At 35 years old, success is to work hard and make more money

At 45 years old, success is to maintain the appearance of a young man – have a good job, a wife, children; and good things of life

At 5o years old success is to provide good education for your children

At 55 years old, success is defined as still being able to perform your duties well at home at work and in the ministry

At 60 years old, success is measured by your ability to still keep your driving license

At 65 years old, success could be defined as living without any kind of disease

At 70 years old, success is when you are not a burden on anyone including your children

Also at 70 years old, success is when you can be thankful daily for the gift of life. Remember that many who had the same birthday with you, did not reach 70 or beyond.

At 75 years old, success is your ability to still have some of your old friends.

At 80 years old, success is when you can know your way back home without being guided or reminded (people tend to forget things as they grow old).

At 85 years old, success is when you do not urinate in your pants again.

At 90 years old success is when you can walk without support again

Indeed! LIFE IS A CIRCLE!

Don't expect too much from it! Live simple! Be happy by force no matter your battles or mistakes. You can't go back and change the beginning, but you can start where you are, and change the ending".

C.S. Lewis.

10. WHEN AM I SUPPOSED TO BE READY FOR MARRIAGE?

Marriage is a life-time relationship, one needs to pray and plan for it. Readiness for marriage has to do with making adequate preparations before going into it. To fail to plan is to plan to fail.

The bible says in Luke 14:28 "Suppose one of you wants to build a tower, won't you first sit down and estimate the cost to see if you have enough money to complete it?"

Some people rush to get married, only to rush out of marriage because they were never prepared for it. The fact that one is physically matured - a girl who has started monthly menstruation, a boy who has started to have nocturnal emission or wet dreams is not a sign of readiness for marriage. Marriage is not just to have a legal permission to relate sexually, it involves a lot of spiritual, financial and social responsibilities that must be properly carried out by husband and wife.

To be ready for marriage you must be:-

Spiritually sound – born again and spirit filled, one who has absolute faith in God and willing to obey God in all things.

Physically matured – between the age of 23 – 26 marriage is neither for a boy and a girl, nor for teenagers, but for a man and a woman.

Educationally sound - Well educated –formally and informally, able to adapt socially and culturally well

Financially independent – have a consistent source of income, versatile and innovative, not relying only on one source

Emotionally stable – a courageous man or woman who will not cry or run away from difficult situations

Socially and morally upright – a good citizen that obeys the laws of the land, and who will always do the right thing.

11. HOW DO I KNOW THE PERSON I AM TO MARRY?

This question may sound funny but it is not. As a child of God, you are in the midst of many suitable sisters but that does not mean you can marry just any of them. I believe God has a specific person He has created for you, you have to pray very well so that you will meet the bones of your own bones and flesh of your flesh.

Know very well that you are to marry a born again Christian, a believer and follower of Jesus Christ and a child of God like you, you cannot afford to marry an unbeliever because it is written two cannot work together unless they agreed, Amos 3:3. "Be ye not unequally yoked together with unbelievers; for what fellowship has righteousness with unrighteousness? And what communion has light with darkness?" 2 Corinthians 6:14. When oxen are unequally yoked, they cannot perform the task set before them. Instead of working together, they will be at odds with one another resulting in a lots of problems.

How do I know her? You have to pray to God to lead and guide you through the Holy Spirit to the woman He has prepared for you. God wants to be involved in even the smallest details of our lives. His Word tells us to commit our ways unto the Lord, acknowledge Him in all our ways, and He will direct our paths. When you pray to God, you should expect Him to speak to you, guide you and give you the desires of your heart. He has a plan for your life and He will lead you to a place of peace. He is your guide, counselor and helper.

You need to hear from God concerning your life partner. Hearing from God will keep you on the right track. God speaks to us in many ways – they include but are not limited to His word, natural things, other people, circumstances, internal peace , wisdom, supernatural revelation, personal conviction, dreams, visions and inner witness best described as a "Knowing deep inside". First and foremost, God speaks to us through His written Word, and every other way that he communicates to us will always agree and never contradicts the Bible.

God will tell you the way to go but you still have to do the walking. Through Christ and the power of His Holy Spirit, God will speak to you, He will lead you step by step to the person He has created for you.

12. CAN I MARRY A WIFE / HUSBAND FROM ANOTHER NATION, TRIBE, OR RACE DIFFERENT FROM MINE?

Many decades ago international, inter-tribal and inter-racial marriages were not very common. Nowadays the whole world has become a global village, such marriages are common and recurrent but not without their challenges of cultural conflicts and differences in values.

As a child of God your number one criteria is to marry a Christian, a believer in Christ by name and in action. It is written –"Be not unequally yoked together with unbelievers: for what fellowship hath righteousness with unrighteousness? And what communion hath light with darkness? 2 Corinthians 6:14.

Therefore, the only marriage forbidden is marriage with an unbeliever and idolater- those who do not know God, those still walking in darkness. They need to come to God through Christ from the kingdom of darkness to the marvelous light of the Lord Jesus.

In the Bible, when Isaac was old enough to marry, Abraham said to his eldest servant under oath –"thou shalt not take a wife unto my son of the daughters of Canaanites among whom I dwell: But thou shall go unto my country, and to my kindred, and take a wife unto my son Isaac". Abraham prayed for the servant for success and God answered his prayers. Genesis 24.

We always use the marriage of Isaac and Rebecca as an example to illustrate the importance of marrying someone with whom you share the same set of faith, belief and value.

13. WHAT STEPS DO I TAKE WHEN ATTRACTED TO A SISTER

It is normal for opposite sex to attract, but do not just walk up to a lady in a carefree manner. You need to pray about it first. When you are convinced beyond reasonable doubt that God is leading you to marry her, go and inform your pastor. Your pastor is to pray and find out if the lady is available for marriage. The pastor will call the lady to tell her that you are interested in her for marriage that she should personally go and pray about it. This procedure may sound old fashioned but it is the best way to go about it.

Some brothers create unnecessary problems for themselves and have been continually embarrassed by asking the hand of married or engaged sisters in marriage. The answer will always be "NO".

If she is convinced that you are for her and she is ready to marry you, she will go back to the pastor. After this, you can boldly approach her having prayed and got the conviction. Both of you will inform your parents and close friends about your intention, now both of you are engaged.

The next step is to continue to pray, inquire, search out and find out more about each other. You will go to your marriage counseling unit to start premarital counselling. Most of the time those who follow this pattern have successful marital relationship.

14. WHAT IS WRONG WITH DATING?

Dating is a worldly affairs and unbiblical, the ideal or acceptable Christian relationship before marriage is courtship. Dating is to be romantically involved with someone. In dating two people meet socially with the aim of assessing the suitability of each other as a prospective marriage partner. There is no serious attachment or commitment. A boyfriend and a girlfriend agree to meet on a particular day for the mutual enjoyment of social activities together on regular basis. Most of the time there is a great tendency to get physically or sexually involved with each other. This is not the plan and purpose of God for marriage partners. It is written "Marriage is honorable in all and the bed undefiled: but whoremongers and adulterers God will judge. Hebrews 13:4.

Online dating – online dating is where people meet and get to know each other over the internet instead of in person. This is also not expedient. You need to see the person you are planning to marry physically face-to-face not just on camera or photo, there are photo tricks, do not marry a stranger. There is also the emotional aspect of marriage relationship which is not available on line.

15. WHAT ARE THE BENEFITS OF GOING THROUGH COURTSHIP BEFORE MARRIAGE?

Courtship is a very important and necessary step before marriage ceremony. It is quite different from dating. Courtship begins when a man and a woman of God have prayed and have been personally convinced that they want to marry each other. It is not a testing period, it is a preparatory period for the two people before starting their marriage life officially with a wedding ceremony in the church. They are going through courtship with the intention to marry. Courtship like marriage is an open secret, not should be hidden – family, church members and friends are aware that the two are going to be married.

During courtship the intending couple will go for premarital counselling which is obligatory. They will have to go through with marriage counsellors every topic on marriage to prepare them for a better married life. This is not a license for them to live together or cohabit. It is not yet time for sexual relationship because they are not yet married. It is time to find out more about each other, the families, what is special about each other, what they have in common and their differences.

It is the time to pray together and plan together with their parents, pastors, fellow Christians about the When? Where? How and What? – of the wedding ceremony. They would have to discuss and agree on where to live, how many children and many other things that will help them settled down well after the wedding.

Most of the time, intended couple who go through courtship and attend premarital counselling make good success of their married life than those who don't.

17. NOT ALL COURTSHIPS END IN MARRIAGE WHY?

Courtship is a very special time for the two people who have prayed and are ready to marry each other. However not all courtships end in marriage because, as we say in counselling – "A broken courtship is better and preferred to a broken marriage. Courtship is a time of sitting down and counting the costs. If after much discussions and deep considerations there are reasons for which any of the two does want to proceed further to marriage it is understandable and acceptable.

In courtship especially during counselling, intended couples are exposed to marriage as ordained by God and the roles of husband and wife in marriage. Investigation about each other goes on as they discuss their future together. If after much discussions and investigations there are cogent reasons why the marriage could not be celebrated, the people involved would have to cut or disengage from the relationship. Nothing is lost at this stage. That is why you are not expected to be physically and emotionally involved before wedding. If you find that your intended spouse has been married before, and the husband and wife is still alive, you cannot marry such a person.

MAKING A CHOICE OF LIFE PARTNER

18. WHY SHOULD MY PASTOR, PARENTS OR ANYONE BE INVOLVED IN MY CHOICE OF MARRIAGE PARTNER?

It is written – "Without counsel purposes are disappointed: but in the multitude of counselors they are established" Proverbs 15:22."…In the mouth of two or three witnesses shall every word be established." 2 Corinthians 12: 1b.

You have the exclusive right to make your own choice of a life partner. Your parents, pastors and friends can only play advisory roles. In any case, it is advisable for you not to choose alone. Your Pastor, parents and others should be told to pray about it. Parents should make their enquiries tactfully about the person. The pastor is your spiritual father, you need his godly counsel and guardian. With your age and education you still have a lot to benefit from the experience and wisdom of your parents and pastor. It will save you a lot of heartaches and disappointments.

19. WHAT QUALITIES SHOULD I LOOK FOR IN A HUSBAND TO BE?

- Must be born again, a genuine Christian in words and in deeds

- A person filled with the Holy Spirit, manifesting the fruits of the Spirit

- A loving, kind and gentle child of God, pleasant and lively to be with

- A humble person, Christ like and godly in Character – character not charisma

- A spiritual, prayerful, full of faith and evangelical Christian living for Christ

- An educated, hardworking, intelligent, skilled and innovative person

- Must be financially capable, dependent and have at least one source of regular

Income – the woman should be able to contribute financially too

- Must be physically strong, not less than 23 years of age

- An emotionally balanced and a mentally stable person

- Should be able to feed himself, wife and children when they arrive – must not depend on parents or in-law to be financially responsible for the family

- A positive, innovative, versatile and visionary person, always looking forward

- Presentable, social, and amiable, someone you will be proud of at any time

- Someone morally upright, holy and heaven conscious

- Someone who has vision and has plans for the future

"Delight yourself also in the Lord and He shall give you the desires of your heart; Commit thy way unto the Lord, trust also in him and he shall bring it to pass" Psalm 37: 5-6.

20. WHEN SHOULD I PROPOSE TO THE SISTER I WISH TO MARRY?

After you have personally prayed and got the conviction that the sister is meant for you. You should also inform your pastor, so that he can pray and find out if the person is available or not. In Christianity you don't just walk up to a sister and say you want to marry her, marriage is more serious and life changing relationship. Talk about marriage proposal only when you are spiritually, physically, financially and emotionally ready for it.

21. HOW DO I PROPOSE? WHAT DO I SAY?

If you have done your homework well, going through the right steps, proposal and what to say will not be a problem, it will come naturally.

Questions such as "I have prayed and I am convinced that you are meant for me, will you marry me?"

"I have always loved and admired you, will you marry me?"

"I believe we can build a home together, will you marry me?

"I would like us to be husband and wife! Please pray about it"

These days some people dramatize it, having gone through the processes, with a ring in hand they kneel to say "Will you marry me?" – The lady will take the ring for a "Yes"! (In RCCG, we do not wed with a ring but with the Holy Bible.

Marriage proposal is an art, there is no hard and fast rule about it. Watch and pray. When the opportunity comes don't miss it.

22. WHAT IF THE LADY SAYS "NO?"

Some of the times the "NO" may be a way of saying – "Give me some time"

"NO" may actually means "I am not for you" If that is the case, there is always a way out. If you have gone through the due process and the answer is "NO", you may need to ask "Why?"

If the reasons are cogent enough, let it go and trust God for the bone of your own bones and the flesh of your flesh.

If the reasons are not genuine enough and you are convinced and persuaded that the lady is for you, be patient and pray more till you have the breakthrough. Pray till your joy is full - Ask, and ye shall receive, that your joy may be full. John 16:24.

23. HOW LONG SHOULD I WAIT FOR AN ANSWER?

Getting an answer should not take too long. If you have prayed and follow due pattern, the answer should not be long. There is need to exercise patience. The lady may want to find out many things about you or want to be sure you are really prepared for marriage.

Once the lady says yes, courtship begins. The time between proposal and courtship should not be more than six months or at most one year. The Bible says "Hope deferred makes the heart sick, but a longing fulfilled is a tree of life" Proverbs 13:12. There is no need to play a hard- to – get game.

24. AS A SISTER HOW DO I SAY "YES" TO A MARRIAGE PROPOSAL FROM A BROTHER WHEN CONVINCED?

It is easier to say "YES" most of the time than to say "NO"

So sister say "YES" in words, deeds or action. The question from intending husband would normally be like "Sister, I hope you are really praying about what we discussed? "Are you now convinced? "Have you received from the Lord concerning our marriage relationship"? "What is the Lord saying about us?" The answer could be any of these -

"Well, we have prayed and the Lord has given me the go – ahead!

"Praise the Lord! The Lord has told me we can marry"

"I think we can marry" "I will marry you" … in words.

In action, you can simply get an expressive card to give to the brother who shows your acceptance or approval for marriage. You can decide to pay an unusual visit to the brother – that means you have agreed to be his wife.

I remember as if it were yesterday when my husband proposed to me. He had sent an expressive card to me on my 21st birthday, with my female intuition, I quickly got a hint that he was up to something. He had been praying anyway and has spoken to our pastor about it before sending signals to me. We were both in the same University of Ife then, now Obafemi Awolowo University and in the same Christian Church – CAC Bethel Church.

He had left the Campus a year earlier and was working at the then Ministry of External Affairs. I have just finished my final year exams, looking forward to going on NYSC. He came from Lagos to personally tell me that I should pray about it, that the Lord was leading him to propose to me as a wife and he was convinced we could build a home together – that informed my first book on marriage "HOME BUILDERS" published in Brasilia, Brazil 1993.

I went to the pastor to tell him about the proposal, he was aware of brother Lawrence's intention. When I told the pastor, he asked me to go and pray about it, and get personal conviction. Before leaving the Campus I went back having prayed myself and with others, that I was convinced I could marry brother Lawrence. Pastor, Professor M. A. Imevbore prayed for me and congratulated me. Just before I left for my NYSC – National Youth Service Corps program, I travelled to Lagos staying with my friend Cordelia, but l never told brother Lawrence that I was coming.

The second day in the evening I visited brother Lawrence, the house was not difficult to locate No 18, Saint Finbarr's street, Akoka, Lagos. On getting there, brother was very happy to see me. I was too shy to say anything. We were just exchanging usual, casual pleasantries. Then I told him l was about leaving, he now became serious and he asked 'Sister Gbemi what about our discussion? What are you saying about it? I was just looking at him laughing.

I now said "Do you think I would travel all the way from Ife to visit you in Lagos to come and say "NO"? We both laughed about it, we knelt down and prayed, committing the courtship unto to the Lord. That was how we started the courtship in the year 1982 that culminated into our wedding on Saturday December 17th at Saint Ursula's Anglican Church, Bern, Switzerland in 1983.

24. WHY DID I TAKE TIME TO TELL YOU THIS STORY?

Because of the evil consequences of choosing alone, not involving your pastors, parents and others, not doing your research about or knowing the person you want to marry before you say "YES".

Many young future leaders –boys and girls have chosen alone, not involving parents, friends and pastors before saying "YES", and they have either died untimely, forcefully separated or divorced, and have become singles again because they discovered they did not know who they say "YES" to.

The blessings of going through due process in choice making –personally praying earnestly and hearing from God, involving pastors, parents, friends in prayers, finding out about the person, not marrying a stranger, not dating, and not visiting sisters or brothers anyhow before marriage can never be over emphasized.

To the young ones outside there, never choose your marriage partner alone! The process is not archaic, it is still in vogue and forever acceptable for those who have the understanding of the fact that marriage is a life-long relationship, you don't enter into it anyhow so that you don't rush out of it anyhow. A word is enough for the wise. Be wise.

25. MY PARENTS ARE PRESSURIZING ME TO MARRY, I DON'T THINK THE MAN IS READY FOR MARRIAGE, HOW CAN I STOP THIS?

To pressurize is to use persuasion or intimidation to make someone do something he or she does not really want to do. When it comes to marriage, refuse to be pressurized into marriage to satisfy the selfish pleasure of anyone, even your parents. Simply tell your mother you are not ready, period! Marriage involves a lot of responsibilities. It is not just to get official permission to relate sexually with a woman, there must be spiritual and financial preparations. Failure to plan is planning to fail.

I have witnessed a situation where a mother coerced her daughter into marriage because she wanted to see her grandchild before she died. The daughter gave in to her persuasion and tears, got married to a husband who could not even take care of himself, talk less of a wife or child.

Not so long after the marriage the mother died. She did not live to see the life of sorrow and regret she pushed her daughter into before her death. The marriage did not just work out!

26. I AM A 28 YEARS OLD CHRISTIAN SISTER, CAN I MARRY A 52 YEAR OLD MAN?

Some people say age is no problem where there is love. There is what we call "generational gap" and it matters in marital relationship. The gap in age between you and this man is too much. Though unwritten, the gap between the age of a man and his wife should not be more than 3 or 5 years. Is like you are marrying someone who is old enough to be your father.

Definitely, there will be generational gap conflicts – the way you think and do things are bound to be different. Another grey area is that by the time your children will need the help of their father financially for educational purposes and others, he would have been retired from whatever service he is into now. How will you take care of your children? They may have to depend on your own salary alone which may not be enough.

Unless you are so desperate to marry, I will advise that you marry someone who is of your own generation. It is possible for the man to find a woman of his own generation too.

27. I HAVE A PROBLEM, I DON'T LOVE THE BROTHER WHO PROPOSED TO ME, BUT I THINK HE IS GENUINE, WHAT SHOULD I DO?

It depends on your own understanding of what love is. Biblically, love is of God. We are told to love one another with the love of God – Agape. Agape is the unconditional love of God and it is the root of all other love such as Philia – love of the brethren, Eros – the erotic love between a husband and wife and Storge or family love between parents and children.

If you are talking about Eros here, you are making a big mistake. A relationship that starts with Eros rarely stands the test of time. You should love this brother first unconditionally with the love of God – Agape. "But God proves His love for us in that while we were still sinners, Christ died for us" Romans 5:8.

As a born again Christian, he is your brother in Christ, "let brotherly love continue" (in Phileo) Hebrews 13:1. If you can accept him in Agape, continue to love in Phileo, if you are meant for him, as you pray and trust God to help you together in marriage you will begin to have good peculiar feelings and attractions for him. You will want to be with him and as you come together you will experience Eros as husband and wife.

When the children begin to arrive, Storge – family love will begin to manifest between you and your children, then the circle is complete. Of course you have to be attracted to the one you want to spend the rest of your life with but don't let Eros be the binding factor. Only Agape is everlasting and that is what makes Christian marriages survive.

28. YOU ALWAYS SAY WE SHOULD INVOLVE PASTORS, PASTORS ARE NOT GOD. MY PASTOR BETRAYED MY TRUST. I HAVE PRAYED AND RECEIVED ABOUT A SISTER, BUT MY PASTOR WANTS ME TO MARRY ANOTHER SISTER – HIS RELATIVE. WHAT AM I TO DO?

What? I believe this is serious! I am happy you realized that pastors are not God. I agree with you. Anyone still in the flesh could be tempted to manipulate things for his or her own benefits. Pastors are God's servants, they are spiritual leaders and shepherd of the flocks of God. But there are different types of pastors. Because one pastor misbehaved should not discourage you. Pastors should not be match makers. They ought to pray and hear from God in every situation.

If you are convinced about a sister and your pastor wants you to marry another one, that may be witchcraft manipulation, it is not of God. You are free to reject such match making. Simply tell your pastor you are not led to marry his choice. You can ask another pastor or a trusted friend to pray with you. Don't go contrary to the plan of God for your life, follow your godly conscience and be guided by the word of God.

29. I AM A GRADUATE BUT THE BROTHER I WANT TO MARRY HAS ONLY A SECONDARY SCHOOL CERTIFICATE OF EDUCATION, CAN WE MARRY?

Yes you can marry if you are both convinced you are meant for each other. That should not be the end of the story educationally anyway. Once you are married, both of you should plan for your husband to improve on his level of education.

There are adult education classes around you can benefit from. This is very important to avoid social and educational complex at home and outside, after your marriage.

Acquisition of knowledge is profitable, knowledge is the raw material for wisdom and understanding. Proverbs 4:7 7 -8 "Wisdom is the principal thing; therefore get wisdom: and with all thy getting get understanding. Exalt her, and she shall promote thee: she shall bring thee to honour, when thou embrace her"

30. I WAS IN A RELATIONSHIP WITH A MAN BEFORE I GOT BORN AGAIN. HE PROMISED TO MARRY ME, AND WITHIN 2 YEARS WE HAD TWO CHILDREN. THIS MAN LATER WALKED OUT ON ME AND MARRIED ANOTHER PERSON IN THE CHURCH. THIS IS THE FIFTH YEAR SINCE I SAW HIM LAST. NOW I HAVE A SUITOR WHO WANTS TO MARRY ME, THE TWO CHILDREN NOT WITHSTANDING, SHOULD I MARRY HIM?

I sympathize with you for being jilted, this kind of situation is very rampant these last days. You ought not to have walked or been so closed to a man outside marriage. The consequences of such error are not palatable at all. Now you have two children outside marriage! I hope the man has not denied their paternity and his responsibilities for them. It is well.

"…The times of this ignorance God winked at, but now commands all men and women everywhere to repent" Acts 17:30.

Your bad behavior in your time of ignorance God has winked at, I believe you have repented of the sin of fornication. You are forgiven and God is covering your past with a willing suitor, our God is merciful. If truly you were never married in the church to this man who deserted you and your children, and you did not do any traditional or in the court marriage, you can marry.

Once beaten, twice shy! I hope you have learned your lessons well from your past relationship. I strongly advise that you keep yourself pure, don't be involved in sexual relationship with this man until you are married in the Church, in the presence of a holy congregation. Also make your investigations very well, find out about this man to be sure he has never married, he is prepared for marriage, and that he is really sincere and genuine.

This time around, don't do it alone. Involve your pastor, your parents and good friends. I wish you well.

31. HOW CAN I KNOW IF THE MAN WHO WANTS TO MARRY ME REALLY LOVES ME?

Love is an abstract emotion, you may not see it physically but you can see it in action. That is why the Bible says that our love should not be by mouth only, love should be in word and in action. If you are familiar with the person before, you would have known a little bit about his character; and this is why you cannot marry a stranger who you do not know anything about. You will find out more during courtship if the person really loves you or not. Read I Corinthians chapter 13, to understand love in action. From the Scriptures we can deduct that someone who loves you will:-

Always be gentle and kind towards you

Will not be proud or boastful or arrogant to you

Will not misbehave himself, will want to do only what pleases you

Will be so caring, so thoughtful and so mindful of you that will always look forward to helping you, doing something good for you or with you

Will not be happy when things are not right with you, will not desert you when you are sick or when things are hard for you

Will be patient with you, endure and if need be suffer for you and with you

Will be accommodating and willing to give you enough room to express yourself, will communicate freely with you, looking forward to hearing you

Will not talk you down, abuse you, make jest of you even when you are wrong or made mistakes, will not shout at you or ridicule you privately or publicly

Will be positive in outlook, always praying, always hoping that all will be well with you

We be willing to go to any length to help you, to make sure you are comfortable and happy with him / her

Will not want to fail or disappoint you, will never be abusive or disrespectful to you

Will believe in you and whatever you say, even when it is clear that something is wrong may not be happy but will not victimize you

Will want you and him /her to rejoice in the truth of the gospel and in doing the right things

Will never force you to have sex, rape you or violate you in any way

Will be ready to defend you at all times, will not be happy to hear bad things about you and will never say bad things about you to others

Will always see the best in you and will never be envious or jealous of your talent, education or status in life

Will be supportive of your goals and objectives, always finding solutions

Not offensive or always using excuses not to get things done for you

The list can continue, by their fruits the Bible says you will know them. The Holy Spirit of God will fill you, God will give you the gift of discerning of Spirit to know when somebody is just loving you by mouth or sincerely in word and in actions.

32. MY PASTOR TOLD ME ABOUT A BROTHER WHO WANTS TO MARRY ME. I HAVE PRAYED VERY WELL AND I AM NOT REALLY CONVINCED THAT I AM MEANT FOR HIM. I PITY THE BROTHER AND I AM FINDING IT DIFICULT TO SAY "NO" TO MY PASTOR. WHAT CAN I DO?

You have the right to reject or accept an offer of marriage. You don't have to say "YES" when you mean to say "NO".

No one should ever marry out of pity, fear, sympathy, to please or to encourage anyone, it does not work. Do not propose or accept an offer of marriage because of "What people will say" "the parents" or "the pastor"- Don't you ever go into a life-long relationship because you think that is what your pastor or anybody wants. It is your life, you are the one getting married. The choice is always yours, any other person can advise you but they have no right to force you to marry anyone. You can always say "NO" if that is what you want.

You remind me of a popular song that we sang in my primary school in the 1960s –   "Wherever you go – go go gongo!

Wherever you be – sisi Eko

Do not say "Yes", when you mean to say "NO"!

Go ahead right now and tell your pastor exactly what you feel and why you feel so. Don't allow yourself to be goaded into any relationship you don't want, that is "witchcraft manipulation". Wait on the Lord for the bone of your bone and the flesh of your flesh – surely the one that is meant for you will come at the right time.

33. WHY IS IT THAT ONLY BROTHERS MAKE MARRIAGE PROPOSAL TO SISTERS? WHY CAN'T A SISTER WHO LOVES A BROTHER TELL HIM SHE WOULD LIKE TO MARRY HIM?

This question though funny is a serious one! It shows to what length the enemy has gone to bastardize and canalized a spiritual phenomenon. Satan, through the sin and the flesh is trying to redefine marriage and he is violating the copy right of God the institutor and founder of marriage.

Marriage is God's idea. It is God who said that it was not good for man to be alone. Evidently it was man that was first created and the woman came from the man. Please Read Genesis Chapter 1. 26 – 31; 2:7, 18-25.

God Himself is the one that arranged the way marriage proposal should be by creating first the man and then brought the woman out of the rib of the man. The man is a whole integer, the woman is to complete and compliment him. The man should be the one to look for his missing rib – not the rib looking for the man.

It is written- therefore shall a man leave his father and his mother and shall cleave unto his wife and they shall be one flesh. It is the man that leaves to cleave to his wife. It is easier for a whole to find a part.

This idea of "a part" looking for a "whole integer" has led to grievous consequences mostly on "the part". When girls begin to look for boys, women looking for men, it is abnormal, it is an aberration. No wonder many of these girls and women get violated, wounded and jilted in the end.

Young and old ones, be obedient to God. It is out of lust for a girl to first say I love you to a boy! You may not take this – it is not natural for a woman to call a man into a relationship, only women of questionable character morally and spiritually do that. The Bible method is archaic? No.

Outdated? No. Acceptable and sociable Yes! Yes! Yes! It is the nature of man to give and the woman to accept or receive. You cannot change the word of God by this new age witchcraft manipulations.

This is why it is Biblically wrong for a woman to wed a man! This is very common, now it is the vogue for a girl to wed a boy. This is unbiblical and this practice should be arrested. The Correct thing to write or say whether in the invitation card or wedding program is –

Lawrence Weds Cecilia   Ayodele Weds Bolanle

This means Lawrence made the proposal, and he is taking Cecilia as a wife. Ayodele has found his missing rib in Omobolanle and He is going to take her as a wife. It is the husband that goes to take a wife in accordance with the Bible please. Let us begin to do it the right way so that it will be as it is supposed to be.

COURTSHIP AND PREMARITAL COUNSELING

____

34. WHAT IS COURTSHIP? HOW DOES IT DIFFER FROM DATING?

Courtship is the preparatory period between the acceptance of marriage proposal and the wedding ceremony. When two people accept to marry each other, they need some period to get to know each other better and plan together for their future as husband and wife. In courtship, an intending couple should go for premarital counseling as they plan towards their engagement and wedding ceremonies. The couple have come together in courtship with the intention to marry.

Dating is a kind of courtship with a difference. A man or woman can agree to go out with two or three persons at the same time to assess each other and determine how compatible they are for marriage. In dating no serious commitment is made towards each other, it is a game that the smartest wins because other relationships are usually hidden. There is high tendency to be physically involved in sex, this casual and carnal relationship may not end in marriage.

35. WHY IS IT COMPULSORY TO GO FOR PREMARITAL COUNSELING?

It is a common saying that when you fail to prepare, you are preparing to fail. Courtship is a time of preparation for wedding and settlement in marriage. Once a man and a woman have prayed, done their investigations about each other very well, and are convinced they can marry each other, they are in courtship, and are engaged to marry.

Premarital counseling is where intended couples are taught, trained, instructed, guided and adequately informed about What? Who? How? When? Where? Dos and Don'ts, Principles and practices of Biblical or Christian marriage. Biblical standard must be followed in Biblical marriage and there should be no controversy or compromise about this if you want to make a success of your marriage – Joshua 1:8 "This book of the law shall not depart out of thy mouth; but thou shalt meditate therein day and night, that thou mayest observe to do according to all that is written therein: for then thou shalt make thy way prosperous, and then thou shalt have good success".

People learn new things, old destructive ideas are deshelled, doubts are cleared, new ways of doing things are embraced, bad habits are put off and good manners are put on. It will surprise you that at times some educated people in literary, art and science are illiterates when it comes to the subject of marriage. Some intelligent people are groping in darkness and they are misbehaving in the field of marriage, why? Because they are uninformed about this special relationship.

The fact that you are going to marry a born again Christian, even a pastor or the most diligent worker in your church does not guarantee success in marriage. You must be informed, instructed and guided by the word of God. That teachings and godly precepts for marital life are done through premarital counseling. This is why more than ever before you have to go through premarital counseling before you say "I Do".

36. HOW LONG SHOULD COURTSHIP LAST?
The Bible says everything has its own time, and there is a specific time for every activity under heaven - Ecclesiastes 3:1. The word of God is forever settled. Nowadays our young generations seem not to be conscious of the fact that there is specific time for every activity in life. Therefore they do what they want, at any time, and how they want it. Because so many of them have put their carts before their horses, their journeys towards marriage have been rough, winding, with little or no progress and some have come to a standstill, they cannot move forward

or go backward regarding marriage and it is affecting their life badly.

Courtship should not start until you are fully prepared and ready for marriage. You must have achieved your educational goals and be a man of a promising career before you think of getting married. There is time for everything brethren, I don't expect a university student who has just gained admission and is in part one of a four - year or three - year course at this level of education to "get engaged"; for what? So you will be courting for three or four years before marriage? That is a very wrong thing to do at this time because it is time to study and get prepared for adulthood. Wait until you have gotten your degree and you don't have to court for long.

Courtship should not be too long or too short. Let us say at least one year if you have been familiar with each other or at most two years if you are strangers to each other. No courtship should be less than six months no matter the situation, because the people involved must go through premarital counseling before wedding.

37. WHAT ARE THE DO'S AND DON'TS OF COURSHIP?

Courtship is a preparatory period for marriage, you are not yet married so don't do what the married are doing. In courtship you are not to:-

- Cohabit or live together

- Be physically or emotionally involved together in sexual intercourse

- Be cooking and eating together as a husband and wife

- Address or tag yourself as husband or wife – you are not yet married

- Meet at night, in secluded places or sleep in each other's house.

Courtship is the time to:-

Pray and fast together, meeting in the church to pray about your future together

Be familiar with each other's family – know your in-laws

Get closer to each other – know each other better, your likes and dislikes, your aims and aspirations in life

Discover what you have in common and how you can serve God together

Discuss and plan towards your engagement and wedding ceremonies

Agree on where to live, how many children to have etc. etc.

38. WHY IS SEX FORBIDDEN FOR PEOPLE IN COURTSHIP?

Because sexual intercourse before marriage is fornication. Fornication is described as the quickest way to hell. God the author of marriage is against fornication.

It is written - Now the body is not for fornication, but for the Lord; and the Lord for the body- I Corinthians 6:13. "Know ye not that the unrighteous shall not inherit the kingdom of God? Be not deceived: neither fornicators….shall inherit the kingdom of God" (1 Corinthians 6:9, 10) "Flee fornication. Every sin that a man does is without the body; but he that commits fornication sins against his own body" (1 Corinthians 6:18).

Sex is the gift of God for the married only, and it is usually the first gift to be unwrapped after the wedding ceremonies are over. "Therefore shall a man leave his father and his mother, and shall cleave unto his wife: and they shall be one flesh and they were both naked, the man and his wife, and were not ashamed". Genesis 2:24 -25.

Sex is for husband and wife, not for fiancé and fiancée, not for boyfriend and girlfriend, and not for Christian Brother and sister that have been engaged to marry. Sex is allowed only in the marriage context. Sex can only be enjoyed mutually and exclusively, without shame on marital bed. Those who are engaged to be married or are in courtship should not have sex. Be warned, God is not mocked, whoever sows to the flesh is bound to reap corruption, avoid it. Moreover, it is written. "Marriage is to be held in honor among all, and the marriage bed is to be undefiled; for fornicators and adulterers God will judge" Hebrew 13:4.

39. WHAT IS THE IMPLICATION OF GETTING MARRIED WITHOUT PARENTAL APPROVAL?

We cannot over-emphasize the idea of getting your parents involved when making a choice of marriage partner. You are under your parental authority until you have your own family. Parent look forward to the wedding of their children, and if there are people who really want it to be well with you in your life, they are your parents. God knows this and that is why He tells children to honor and obey their parents in the Lord in all thing.

"Children, obey your parents in all things: for this is well pleasing unto the Lord. Colossians 3:20 - Children, obey your parents in the Lord: for this is right Ephesians 6:1. - Honour thy father and thy mother: that thy days may be long upon the land which the LORD thy God giveth thee Exodus 20:12.

When it comes to marriage, you have the right to choose, but don't do it alone, involved your parents, pastor and others in prayers and counseling. If for any reason your parents say they don't want you to marry someone or they prefer someone else, you must ask them why? Your parents will tell you the truth without fear or favour. Parents are more experienced, at times they see what younger generation cannot see and they are conscious of deep things in marriage more than youthful exuberant.

Find out from your parents the reasons for their disapproval. Pray about it, you can engage their friends or close relatives to plead with them for you. Don't be too much in a hurry to marry without the blessings of your parents. If you do, you are a woman or man stealer, no thief will enter heaven. So wait, be patient, pray and get the approval of your parents before you marry.

40. I AM GREATLY DISAPPOINTED IN THE CHURCH AND MY PASTOR. I AM A FAITHFUL COMMITED MEMBER OF OUR CHURCH. UNFORTUNATELY, DURING COURTSHIP I HAD AN AFFAIR WITH MY FIANCEE AND WE CONFESSED TO OUR PASTOR. I WAS GREATLY EMBARRASSED WHEN THE PASTOR

TOLD US THAT OUR WEDDING PLAN HAS BEEN CANCELED. I KNOW MANY IN THE SAME CHURCH WHO DID THE SAME THING BUT DID NOT CONFESS, SOME EVEN HAD ABORTION AND THEY WERE MARRIED IN THIS CHURCH. IS THIS NOT PARTIALITY AND DISCRIMINATION IN THE CHURCH? WHY SHOULD THAT BE?

Dear brother in Christ I really admire and commend your courage and sincerity. The Bible says in the book of Proverbs chapter 28 verse 14 –"He that covereth his sins shall not prosper: but whoso confesseth and forsaketh them shall have mercy"

Please don't be bitter against the church and your pastor, you may not have obtained their mercy concerning your proposed wedding now, but 1 know God will have mercy on you as you have confessed and repented of your sin of fornication. There is a standard, a Biblical principle to follow in this situation and I know your pastor and church authority have done the right thing. They have corrected and disciplined you in love, though painful now, God will honor and prosper you for not covering your sin.

Your wedding plan was cancelled to serve as a warning for others who are planning to wed like you, and to discourage them from committing the sin of fornication. You are disciplined so that you can build your marriage on a godly, solid foundation. "If the foundation is faulty, what can the righteous do? Psalm 11:3. A faulty foundation is a very dangerous thing, a lot of believers suffer a great deal in marriage because of compromised or faulty foundation. When your foundation is faulty, you have no option but to struggle in life. I hope you have told all the truth, I hope the sister is not pregnant. In any case your wedding that is cancelled can still be done.

Usually, when you have been disciplined like that, and you accept it, your wedding will still take place. Another date will be arranged for you but the wedding may not be as glamorous as you had wanted it to be. If the sister is pregnant, there will be no wedding until she is delivered of the baby or babies. Marriage is between a man and a woman not for three persons. After the delivery, you can now have a Marriage Blessing, done in the vestry and with just few people.

Don't bother yourself about those who cover their sin, God is not mocked, they have their consequences to face sooner or later. I just want to say there is no justification for abortion, it is murder! For someone to be pregnant before marriage is a sin and to now commit abortion is grievous. Do not abort, you stand the risk of losing your life or damaging your reproductive system. Be careful, be godly. You may choose to do whatever you like, but you will not be able to choose your consequences, as you prepare your bed, so you will lay on it.

41. WHY IS GETTING PREGNANT BEFORE MARRIAGE NOT ALLOWED IN OUR CHURCH?

Because it is a sin, it is a worldly idea, unbiblical and it is building the marriage on a faulty foundation. Child bearing is not the first and only reason for marriage. The first reason for marriage is to solve the problem of loneliness, to have a place of fellowship. God has given the married couple the authority to be fruitful and multiply- Genesis 1:28. No one will be barren in marriage according to the plan of God "no one shall suffer miscarriage or be barren in your land; I will fulfill the number of your days." Exodus 23:26.

Having children out of wedlock is not the plan and purpose of God for marriage. Children should be conceived and born after the wedding ceremony not before it. No child of God should entertain fear about being barren or allow herself to be pressurized into getting pregnant before marriage.

42. IS IT GOOD TO MARRY A SINGLE WOMAN WHO ALREADY HAS A CHILD OUT OF WEDLOCK?

There are many different types of singles - never married, widowed, separated, divorced, jilted or disappointed, single fathers and single mothers. There is nothing bad in getting married to a single mother who was never married. She may have been impregnated by a boy or man friend who was not prepared to be a father. However, you need to know the reason why the lady did not marry the father of her child.

If you are comfortable with her situation and explanation, the present should inform the future not her past. Remember "There is therefore now no condemnation to them which are in Christ Jesus, who walk not after the flesh, but after the Spirit. Romans 8:1; 4:8 Blessed are they whose iniquities are forgiven, and whose sins are covered."

43. WHY DO WE HAVE TO GO FOR A BLOOD AND PREGNANCY TESTS BEFORE WEDDING?

Many unthinkable scenarios are happening even in the church in these last of the last days. Perilous time is really here, more than ever before Pastors and marriage committee members should be more watchful and prayerful before joining two people in marriage. Never join a couple suddenly no matter how the pressure. A lot of deceit is going on out there and you must be very careful not to partake of other people's sin by joining those that are not supposed to be joined.

There are precepts for the Christian marriage and specific standard to follow. The tests you are going to do are for your own good, to save you from harrowing, complicated, and life destroying circumstances in the future.

BLOOD TEST- You have to do blood tests to confirm your:-

HIV status - What Is HIV? Acquired immunodeficiency syndrome – (AIDS) is a virus that attacks cells that help the body fight infection, making a person more vulnerable to other infections and diseases. It is spread by contact with certain bodily fluids of a person with HIV, most commonly during sex.

Sickle – cell anemia – a parental inherited condition in which there aren't enough healthy red blood cells to carry adequate oxygen throughout the body. Problems in sickle cell disease typically begin around 5 to 6 months of age. A number of health problems may develop, such as attacks of pain, anemia, swelling in the hands and feet, bacterial infections and stroke. Two people with sickle – cell anemia should not marry because of the bad health conditions.

Covid 19 – Corona virus status – this is a recent 9December 19) but very deadly virus infection that originated in Wuhan, China but is now all over the world. Thousands of people have died of it despite the social and physical lock down all over the world.

If any of you tests positive for any of these blood anomalies, you will not be allowed to marry. This test should be done very early in courtship, there will be no need to continue in the relationship because it will not end in marriage.

PREGNANCY TEST – This is very important to be sure that the wife - to - be is not pregnant. In these last days, people who are in courtship have high tendency to be involved sexually before their wedding. As if that were not bad enough, some get pregnant and they would now rush to get married. After six or seven month you will hear that the wedding you conducted six months ago, the bride has put to bed! To crown this shame with hypocrisy, they will say the baby came prematurely. Of course we were not born yesterday. That is why pastors should not rush to wed people. You must give at least six month notice, the ideal is one year. This test should be done in a private, designated hospital. The result should be sent directly to the marriage committee, not through the intending couple to avoid manipulations.

44. AFTER OUR WEDDING, I DISCOVERED THAT MY HUSBAND HAS TWO CHILDREN WITH HER FORMER GIRL FRIEND AND HE NEVER TOLD ME THIS BEFORE. NOW THE FAMILY IS BEGGING ME TO ACCEPT THE CHILDREN TO LIVE WITH ME AND MY HUSBAND BUT I HAVE REFUSED, WHAT DO YOU

THINK I SHOULD DO? I AM STILL TRUSTING GOD FOR THE FRUIT OF THE WOMB.

In reality your husband did not behave well by not letting you know he has gotten children outside wedlock. That tantamounts to a fraud. Your husband should be humble and kind enough to accept his fault and sincerely apologize to you for that. Pray for the grace to forgive and forget, don't allow the past mistake of your husband to ruin your marriage. The Lord will comfort and uphold you in the name of Jesus. Amen.

These children are innocent and they need mother care. If their mother would be willing to release them to live with you, it would be a great opportunity to show the love of God to those children as you look forward to having your own biological children. There must be a reason why the family is begging you to help your husband take care of those children. It may be that their mother is incapable and you are better placed.

In this kind of situation you have to be very patient, pray and trust God to divinely intervene. Ask the Holy Spirit to comfort you and guide you to do the right thing concerning these children. If it is possible to let the children come, please allow them for Christ's sake - And the King shall answer and say unto them, Verily I say unto you, Inasmuch as ye have done it unto one of the least of these my brethren, ye have done it unto me.

The advantage of having the children with you is that the mind of their father – your husband with be at home with you. Your husband will not need to be visiting them somewhere else, or have to see their mother because of them – divided attention! By the time your own children come, it will be a delight to train them, raise them up together in the way of the Lord.

On the other hand if you have a cogent reason why you should not allow them to live with you, have a heart – to-heart discussion   with your husband and let the family know about it.

45. HOW MANY TYPES OF WEDDING CEREMONY DO WE HAVE? WHICH OF THESE IS OBLIGATORY FOR A CHRISTIAN?

From the cradle to the grave life is full of ceremonies. When a child is born, he is celebrated at the naming ceremony. There will be a lot of birthday anniversary celebrations and graduations before wedding. Wedding however is very unique because it is the celebration of two people becoming one. No one is ever conscious of naming ceremony or burial ceremony. That is why I always want this unique celebration to be ceremoniously celebrated.

There are three socially acceptable wedding ceremonies –

Traditional or cultural marriage ceremony – Marriage according to cultural or traditional rites depending on the customs and practices of the people involved – celebrated at home or special events places.

 Legal or court marriage – marriage according to the law of the land – celebrated in the court.

Church Wedding (White wedding) wedding according to Christian precepts – celebrated in the church.

A Christian can celebrate all the three. The most important of all is the church wedding. As a Christian you should be married in the church – the house of God. Marriage ceremony should be done in the church, not hotel, not just any hall or any event place. There is also the altar factor that shields you and speaks for your family when you wed in a church. Receptions – the entertainment after the church wedding service could be done in hotel halls and event places.

46. WHOSE CHURCH SHOULD THEY USE FOR THE WEDDING? HUSBAND'S OR WIFE'S?

Scenes of life always change. The only thing that is permanent in human life is change. Not too long time ago, wedding service would take place in the church of the wife, and in her home town. But now things have changed. Most especially the economic situation of most societies has affected where and how people celebrate nowadays.

The husband is supposed to leave his own family and go to bring his wife from her own family. That is why church wedding takes place in the wife's parents' church. What happens now is that both husband and wife could be of the same church in a city, while their parents live in different towns. The families may decide to use the couple's church for the wedding to safe time, energy and money.

I would like to say that church wedding is obligatory for a child of God because of what we call "Altar factor" in the church. An altar is where people meet with their God. An altar is a structure upon which offerings such as sacrifices are made for religious purposes. Altars are found at shrines, temples, churches and other places of worship. Every church has an altar. It is before this erected altar that the couple would be joined together and presented as husband and wife after the wedding.

The church is called the house of God, a place of worship. We know the altar there is a sacred one and we have our pulpits erected at the altar. We know the God we meet at the altar in the church, we bring to our God sacrifice of praise, thanksgiving, offering, tithe, dedication every time we gather. The Pastor officiating at the altar holy altar is bound to speak good things into the life of the couple, their life, marriage and future together are committed into the God of the Altar before whom they are wedded, knowingly or unconsciously.

I am sorry for those who now go for "Location Wedding" – wedding outside the church building at home and abroad, getting married at an unknown altar, dedicating their lives to gods and goddesses. Some of these altars outside the church are dedicated to Satan, demons and territorial strongmen! Don't go there! They are not of God. Such altars should be cried against! - "And he cried against the altar in the word of the LORD, and said, O altar, altar, thus saith the LORD; Behold, a child shall be born unto the house of David, Josiah by name; and upon thee shall he offer the priests of the high places that burn incense upon thee, and men's bones shall be burnt upon thee". I King 13:2.

May the blood of Jesus cry and speak against every evil altar raised against your life and marriage in the name of Jesus.

47. WEDDING INVOLVES A LOT OF EXPENSES, WHO IS RESPONSIBLE? HUSBAND OR WIFE?

It is written – "And the rib, which the LORD God had taken from man, made he a woman, and brought her unto the man. 23 And Adam said, This is now bone of my bones, and flesh of my flesh: she shall be called Woman, because she was taken out of Man. 24 Therefore shall a man leave his father and his mother, and shall cleave unto his wife: and they shall be one flesh". Genesis 2: 22-25.

The husband is the initiator, the one who goes to look for his missing rib and after she has found her gave her a name after himself – "Womb man" shortened to woman. When Abraham sent his servant to get a wife for his son Isaac, the servant did not go empty handed. When Rebecca was taken from her parents she was given a lot of gifts –"And the servant brought forth jewels of silver, and jewels of gold, and raiment, and gave them to Rebecca; he gave also to her brother and to her mother precious things, and they did eat and drink…" Genesis 24: 53.

Biblically, marriage is celebrated with pomp and pageantry, with a lot of food and drinks with happiness and joy. The husband should be prepared to bear the cost of most of the wedding expenses. He should buy gifts for his wife – these are received at the engagement or traditional ceremony. In fact a list of items is given to the groom – engagement list. He will buy clothes, box, shoes, food items etc. etc. to be given to his wife and parents. That is why you must be financially prepared before you get married. Parents of the groom will support him, also the parents of the wife and the wife will also contribute their quotas toward the success of the wedding ceremonies. DON'T BORROW MONEY TO WED. You will be laying a faulty foundation. Use whatever you have, cut your coat according to your material. You will not have any regrets.

48. IS IT COMPULSORY TO HAVE A RECEPTION AFTER A WEDDING CEREMONY?

The way some people are celebrating wedding unceremoniously is disappointing and a kind of an insult to the marriage institution. I have heard about a wedding where the husband and wife just wore simple clothes, no congregation to witness, no program of event, no photograph and of course no entertainment. The hired pastor just did the joining and prayed for them. No music, no dancing! Why? Because they had no money for all such things! So, they have just come to get official permission to be sleeping with each other! I feel this is not good at all.

Do not marry until you are able to marry. Marriage is not for lazy minded, unserious and uncommitted people. Marriage is a relationship that is full of responsibilities, you must be prepared to face them. You don't have to invite the whole town or church to your wedding but at least, let people around know that something good is happening to you on your wedding day.

You are obliged to give food and drinks to your wedding guests after the church wedding. That is what happens at the reception. Remember the marriage at Cana in Galilee, where Jesus turned water into wine? – John 2:1 – 11. Food and drinks are part and parcel of a wedding ceremony. The Lord will help you and make a way for you. You will not be put to shame in the name of Jesus.

49. WHY DO I NEED TO WRITE A WEDDING CHECK LIST?

A wedding check list can also be called a wedding to do list. This is a list that is drawn by a man and woman in preparation to their wedding ceremony. During premarital counselling, the counselor(s) will encourage the counselees to have a paper and begin to jot down all they intend to do before wedding, on wedding day, at the reception and after the reception.

The first and foremost is when the wedding ceremony is coming up.- the Date, time, where, and how? Wedding costumes – Suit for groom and groom men; and best man, white flowing gown for the bride, beautiful gown for the best lady and flower girls. Symbols such as the rings and Bible are essential. Reception - Entertainment – food and drinks, where to cook and pack food? Who bakes the cake? Church program – officiating ministers, the choir? Hymns and choruses? Bible texts? Photographs and video recording; Souvenirs to give to guests at the reception.

You need to arrange for transportation – the cars to take husband and wife to church separately – decorated with "About to Wed" and the Car that will take both of them to the reception after the church – decorated with "Just Married". Plan for your honey moon – where? Which hotel? For how many days? The house you will return to after the wedding? Food stuff to keep for at least one week when you return from honey moon. You have to list them and begin to check them every time to make sure you have taken car for everything needful.

Dear husband and wife don't be anxious about it, God will do it. "Be careful for nothing; but in everything by prayer and supplication with thanksgiving let your requests be made known unto God. 7 And the peace of God, which passeth all understanding, shall keep your hearts and minds through Christ Jesus." Philippians 4:6-7

50. WHAT IS THE IMPORTANCE OF HONEY MOON?

Honey moon is a traditional holiday taken by newlyweds immediately after their wedding. It marks the beginning of a new era and life in togetherness. After the hustling and bustling of the preparation for wedding, wedding service and reception, the couple would have been very tired, they need rest. They need to be relaxed and begin to know each other physically and emotionally. It is the time to enjoy sex as a married couple. Honey moon will afford them this time of intimacy they desire.

It is written – " When a man hath taken a new wife, he shall not go out to war, neither shall he be charged with any business: but he shall be free at home one year, and shall cheer up his wife which he hath taken." Deuteronomy 24:5

AFTER THE WEDDING CEREMONIES

51. WHAT ARE THE IMPLICATIONS OF MARITAL VOWS?

What is a vow? A vow is a solemn promise to perform a specified act, or behave in a certain manner; especially a commitment to live and act in accordance with laid down rules and regulations. Marriage vows are the promises a couple make to each other during their marriage or wedding ceremony to express their obligations and commitment to each other as husband and wife for life.

Marriage as ordained by God is a lifelong relationship. According to the word of God, only death can separate husband and wife. Marriage is also a covenant – an agreement between two parties which involves obligations towards each other. That is why any man of God given the opportunity to join a husband and wife will first call the attention of the couple to the seriousness of what they are a – " I call your attention to the seriousness of the decision which you have made and the covenant you are about to declare before God. The vows you are about to take are not to be taken without careful thought, for in them you are committing yourselves exclusively to one another for as long as you both shall live"

Then the pastor will continue the joining process with the marriage vows as follows

Wedding Vows

If you are ready to assume the obligations and duties before God, as I have defined them, you will unite your hands and pledge your love and your lives to each other.

Groom, repeat after me. I ____, take you, _____, to be my lawfully wedded wife, to have and to hold, from this day forward, for better, for worse, for richer, for poorer, in sickness and in health, to love, cherish and obey, according to God's holy law and this is my solemn vow.

Now Bride, please repeat after me. I _____, take you, _____, to be my husband, to have and to hold, from this day forward, for better, for worse, for richer, for poorer, in sickness and in health, to love, cherish and obey, according to God's holy law and this is my solemn vow.

After this, the two are joined as husband and wife in marriage, and the union sealed with prayers.

The implication of these vows is that once taken, they are seriously binding. The promises made before God and the Holy Congregation who witnessed the event must be fulfilled in all ramifications. Husband and wife must do what they say they would do as long as both of them are alive. Wedding vows are also a great resource for understanding what marriage entails – an unpredictable yet indissoluble lifelong partnership.

Marital vows are declarations before God and man assuring that husband and wife will do as they have promised. There are so many versions of marital vows today but I chose to go by the traditional one.

"I" – When you say "I" – you are saying you were not forced to take this man or this woman as a marriage partner, you are not under any duress but you are consciously taking the man or woman as a life partner. No other person should ever influence you to change your mind or do anything contrary to this person.

"For better" – this implies you will continue to love this person when life is good. It means no spiritual, career, political, economic or educational upliftment, appointment or promotion will affect your love negatively for this person. When riches come, he or she must not suddenly be "below your standard" "Unable to cope or does not match" your new status. This means that you cannot abandon your spouse when riches multiply. The riches are to make the marriage sweeter and not to tear both of you apart

"For worse" Life is not a bed of Roses without thorns, time changes, people can change and situation can also change. If it happens that things go downwards after your wedding, it could be as bad as being involved in adultery, loss of job, power and position. The vow implies that you will continue with the relationship. All you need is to confront, confess and repent, seek for solution through counseling and prayers.

For richer – for poorer – In riches, in poverty. You may experience financial reverses, or total knock out into bankruptcy. Wife do not leave your husband for a greener pastures or better conditions because you can no longer afford some luxuries you were used to before. Husband do not be deceived by money bags women who will promise you financial breakthrough and fulfill it but ask you to leave your family for them. The husband does not need to be too harsh or take it out on the wife, frustrating all her efforts, simply because she is asking for money to meet the needs in the home. Both of you should fast and pray for a divine intervention. Cry unto God and trust Him altogether and things will change for better

In sickness – In health- Many contemporary vows have omitted this idea of being sick, and that may be why some spouses abandon their partners in sickness. Nobody wants or prays to be sick but in reality sickness and diseases are part of human life. Singles as well as married people fall sick for different reasons. Marriage partners have fallen sick, some have been attacked with serious life – threatening sicknesses such as impotency, epilepsy, insanity, barrenness and paralysis after wedding. You vowed to be there for your partner. This is not the time to dump your spouse for another person or run away entirely from home. It is the time to demonstrate the promised commitment made on your wedding day.

Job says "Although affliction cometh not forth of the dust, neither doth trouble spring out of the ground; yet man is born unto trouble, as the sparks fly upward".

When sickness comes all you need to do is what Job did, trust in the faithfulness and the omnipotence of God, call upon you in prayers and He will divinely heal the sick and bring you out of trouble. –"I would seek unto God, and unto God would 1 commit my cause; which doeth great things and unsearchable, marvelous things without number" – Job 6 -9

"Love, Cherish and obey." Love should not only be in words but in action. – Love is kind and suffers a lot. True love is gentle and cares. People in love easily talk, listen and hear each other, they are ready to obey and do anything for each other in love. True love covers a lot of mistakes, disappointments, hardships and failures. Enduring, persevering love will see you through. Nothing should separate husband and wife from the love of God that knits their hearts together. In all life's situations, they are more than conquerors through Christ.

Till death do us part – Only death can dissolve marital vows. No changes in life, no health conditions, no other human being should separate husband and wife, only death – the opposite of life can put an end to a marriage - " So they are no longer two, but one flesh. Therefore what God has joined together, let no one separate." Matthew 19:6. It means that marriage comes from God, and therefore people should not end a marriage, and husband and wife should be faithful to their promises.

QUESTION 52

WHAT ARE THE SIGNIFICANCES OF THE CHRISTIAN WEDDING

CEREMONY SYMBOLS? WHY ARE THEY IMPORTANT?

A wedding is a joyous ceremony where a man and a woman are joined together to become husband and wife. Like me, may be you have witnessed weddings throughout your life. I have celebrated and witnessed many traditional weddings or engagements, court weddings and church weddings- also known as white wedding. The one I like most is the church wedding which takes place inside church building. I wonder if as we celebrate and witness these weddings, we ever thought about the meaning or significance of the costumes and symbols involved.

A symbol is an emblem, something visible that represents something tangible and more significant. For example a dove is a symbol of peace. Christian wedding is celebrated with pomp and pageantry, always full of decisive steps, signs and symbols. Special garments are worn by the bride and groom, the couple enters into the church hall at different time with styles, and vows are made to each other. These symbols are very important because of what they stand for, and a ceremony without the presence or use of these symbols will not be a wedding ceremony.

At the right time in the ceremony, there is the use of the Bible or wedding rings in joining, there will be a presentation of husband and wife after joining, special songs, hymns, and choruses are sang, the marriage certificate will be signed by the couple, parents and appointed delegates with style. Many prayers are offered to God on behalf of the couple, and the church ceremony is usually followed by a wedding reception. Indeed wedding is a ceremonial event. It should not be done shoddily, carelessly or unceremoniously. Wedding should never be void of the necessary costumes and symbols because of their meaning or significances.

Wedding is also a covenant union of two people - husband and wife, with binding obligations towards each other. Many traditional wedding customs have their roots in the ancient and sacred covenant that God made with Abraham. Wedding ceremonies in both the Old and New Testament had distinctly devout and spiritual dimensions because faith in God was woven into the daily fabric of the Hebrew family life. Each covenant has blood as a seal. The covenant of marriage too is sealed and consummated in sexual union where the couple exchange their blood. Knowing the biblical and social significance of these wedding signs and symbols make this special day in the life of the bride and groom more meaningful, unforgettable and memorable.

THE COSTUMES

THE WHITE WEDDING GOWN- Bridal outfits are extremely important in church wedding, especially the wedding dress for the bride and groom. The white wedding dress of the bride has a twofold significance. It is a symbol of the wife's purity in heart and life, as well as her reverence to God. It's also a picture of the righteousness of Christ described in Revelation 19:7-8 "Let us be glad and rejoice, and give honour to him: for the marriage of the Lamb is come, and his wife hath made herself ready. 8 And to her was granted that she should be arrayed in fine linen, clean and white: for the fine linen is the righteousness of saints"

THE SPECIAL SUIT AND ATTRACTIVE APPEARANCE OF THE GROOM-

The groom is a symbol of Christ. Ephesians 5:23-32 reveals that earthly marriages are a picture of the church's' union with Christ. God initiated the relationship through Christ, who called and came for his bride - the church. In this ceremony the man is a type of Christ the bridegroom of the church. In his death and resurrection Jesus Christ established the New Testament covenant, sealed with His blood as   initiated by God in the Old Testament – Genesis 3: 15.   The groom has come to take his bride already adorned and prepared for him. This is the reason the groom enters the church first, looking forward to receiving the bride.

THE VEIL- Bridal veils are used so the groom could not see the face of the bride before the wedding. The most popular belief is that the traditional bridal veil was worn to conceal the bride's beauty .Consequently, the veil could not be lifted up until after the marriage had been solemnized. The woman's veil is also pinned above her head. This means she must submit herself to the leadership of her husband as was written in Ephesians 6.

Not only does the bridal veil show the modesty and purity of the bride and her reverence for God, it reminds us of the temple veil that was torn in two when Christ died on the cross. Removing the veil took away the separation between God and man, giving believers access into the very presence of God. Since Christian marriage is a picture of the union between Christ and the church, we see another reflection of this relationship in the removal of the bridal veil. Through wedding ceremony, the couple now has full access to one another physically and emotionally.

BRIDES'S MAIDS – It is customary for the friends of the bride to rejoice with the bride on her special day. They are for encouragement and support and to adorn the bridal party. Among the maids –between six or eight girls, she has a chief bride's maid who will wait on her and attend to her needs on this special day. It makes the attending bride's maids to look forward to their own wedding day as well.

GROOMS MEN – What the maids are to the bride so are the groom's men to the groom. They are there for encouragement, support, and security of both bride and groom. There is also a special man out of the groom named the "Best Man", he is to wait on the groom and attend to his needs throughout the ceremonies till everything is over. Sometimes the best man and the groom wear the same suit. The dressing of the groom at this royal occasion should be un-mistakenly outstanding. He is the special reason for the ceremony – he is taking a wife.

PAGE BOYS AND FLOWER GIRLS – They are very young children chosen to adorn the bridal party with their beautiful, fanciful dresses and small baskets of flowers. They are little version of the bridesmaids and groom's men. The children – boys and girls symbolize future children of the couple. The authority given to the bride and groom to be fruitful and multiply will be fulfilled in their marriage as represented by these children.

BRIDAL BOUQUET OF FLOWER - Flowers symbolize the aroma of love and fecundity, fertility, increase or fruitfulness. Consequently, the bridal bouquet symbolizes joyful lovemaking and fertility. The ribbons around the flowers symbolize unity and wholeness. Throwing the bouquet at the end of the reception is a recent innovation. Whoever catches it hopes to be the next bride.

WEDDING BELLS – Church bells used to ring loud and clear in my home town of Okun – Owa, in Ogun state of Nigeria. They were very important signs or alerts to us. It was a way to spread the news of an event that occurred in the church – whether it was announcing a service, funeral or wedding. The bells were thought to bring luck and fortune to the newlyweds. It is also believed that the bells summon angels. The church bells would be rung as the couple walked down the aisle together or came out of the church. The wedding bells are often rung today only in orthodox churches as part of the wedding ceremony, to begin and end the service.

With the history of wedding bells and their meaning of love and a new life, couples often choose to theme their wedding around the symbol. Bell representations can be used throughout the wedding - As a graphic on wedding invitation cards, on the wedding programs, as an alternative to pew bows, hung from the ceiling at the wedding reception as part of the wedding reception decoration and on top of the wedding cake. The bells continue to symbolize love, joy, and the start of a new life together for couples who get married.

CUSTOMIZED WEDDING PROGRAM – It is an emblem of the reality of the wedding, a witness to the fact that the wedding actually took place. This is the program of event for the wedding day. It is specially made for the couple, stating their names, the date and venue of wedding. Their chosen hymns and bible passages are well arranged in the booklet and the names of officiating ministers are indicated. This pamphlet may contain the order of service in the church and that of the reception after the church service.

WEDDING RINGS - The wedding ring is a perfect circle, with no beginning and no end. It symbolizes union, permanency, and completeness. Perhaps this is one of the most popular wedding symbols in the whole marriage ceremony. Wedding rings symbolizes love and fidelity for the marrying couple. The ring's roundness is said to represent the eternal love they have for each other. Please note that in RCCG and some churches in Nigeria, they prefer to wed with the Holy Bible alone.

THE CEREMONIES

SEATING OF THE FAMILIES - In biblical times, the parents of the bride and groom were ultimately responsible for discerning God's will concerning the choice of a spouse for their children – example of Abraham arranging the wedding of Isaac and Rebecca. Genesis 24. The wedding tradition of seating the parents in a place of prominence is meant to recognize their responsibility for the couple's union.

Christian marriage is a covenant relationship. The wedding ceremony itself is a picture of the blood covenant between God and mankind. Family and friends of the bride and groom are seated on opposite sides of the church to symbolize their entering into a covenant. The two families are on holy ground, in the house of God and in the presence of God. These family, friends, and invited guests are not just witnesses, they also are participants or stake holders in the wedding covenant. Many have made sacrifices to help prepare the couple for marriage and support them in their holy union. They should be well seated and their comfort should be properly taken care of during the ceremony in the church and at the reception.

FATHER ESCOURTING AND GIVING AWAY THE BRIDE - In Jewish tradition, it was the father's duty to present his daughter in marriage as a pure virgin bride. As parents, the father and his wife also took responsibility for endorsing their daughter's choice in a husband. By escorting her down the aisle, a father says, "I have done my very best to present you, my daughter, as a pure bride. I approve of this man as your choice for a husband, and now I bring you to him." When the minister asks, "Who gives this woman?" the father responds – "I do" or "Her mother and I." This giving away of the bride demonstrates the parents' blessing on the union and the transfer of care and responsibility to the husband. The parents of the bride hands over the right hand of the bride to the officiating pastor, who give it to the groom.

JOINING RIGHT HANDS - In a wedding, as the bride and groom face one another to say their vows, they join right hands and publicly commit everything they are, and everything they possess, in a covenant relationship. They leave their families, forsake all others, and become one with their spouse- Genesis 2: 24; "And said, for this cause shall a man leave father and mother, and shall cleave to his wife: and they twain shall be one flesh? Wherefore they are no more twain, but one flesh. What therefore God hath joined together, let not man put asunder" Mathew 19: 5-6.

WEDDING VOWS - This is the most solemn and important moment of the ceremony. Although every moment of a Christian wedding is important, this is the central focus of the service.

During the vows, the two individuals make a promise to one another publicly, before God and the witnesses present, to do everything within their power to help each other grow to become what God has created them to be, despite all adversities, and as long as they both live. It is a sacred vow, expressing the entrance into a life-long covenant relationship.

EXCHANGE OF RINGS - The exchange of rings expresses the couple's promise of commitment and faithfulness to each other. The unending circle of the ring is a symbol of eternity. The wedding ring is the outward expression of the inward bond, as two hearts unite as one, promising to love each other with fidelity for all eternity. Wearing of the wedding rings throughout the couple's lifetime will tell all others of their commitment to be faithful and loyal to their vows. A ring also represents resources. When the couple exchanges wedding rings, it symbolizes the giving of all their resources—wealth, possessions, talents, emotions—to each other in marriage.

Sample – Exchange of the Rings

Minister: "May I have the rings. Let us pray. Bless, O Lord, the giving, and receiving of these rings. May ___ and ___ abide in Thy peace and grow in their knowledge of your presence through their loving union. May the seamless circle of these rings become the symbol of their endless love and serve to remind them of the holy covenant they have entered into today to be faithful, loving, and kind to each other. Dear God, may they live in your grace and be forever true to this union. Amen."

Groom: "____, I give you this ring as a symbol of our vows, and with all that I am, and all that I have, I honor you. In the name of the Father, and of the Son, and of the Holy Spirit. With this ring, I thee wed."

Bride: "____, I give you this ring as a symbol of our vows, and with all that I am, and all that I have, I honor you. In the name of the Father, and of the Son, and of the Holy Spirit. With this ring, I thee wed."

THE BIBLE – Traditional ceremonies often have the Bride's Bible as part of the gifts for the bride. Nowadays, some Pentecostal churches only use the Bible to join couples in the church. Their rings may be blessed and could be exchanged at the reception. The Holy Bible is the Word of God. It is the Christian's handbook for life. God's message to humanity — his love letter — is contained in the pages of the Bible.

All Scripture is God-breathed and is useful for teaching, rebuking, correcting and training in righteousness...2 Timothy 3:16. The Bible is more powerful than man made rings in keeping husband and wife together forever, and making a success of their marriage – "This Book of the Law shall not depart from your mouth, but you [] shall meditate in it day and night, that you may observe to do according to all that is written in it. For then you will make your way prosperous, and then you will have good success"   Joshua   1:8.

Please note that in a typical Jewish wedding, the couple jointly smash an empty bottle with their feet to symbolize eternal unity.

THE UNITY CANDLE – (MOSTLY IN THE CATHOLIC CHURCH)

According to the book of Mathew chapter 5, we Christians are giving the title '"light of the world". As the groom and the bride have professed that they are followers of Christ, this then implies that each one's life serves as a light to the people around them. But, as a married couple, and as their lives are united, their marriage and their Christian home will now serve as the light, and the example, for the people and families they get in touch with.

This means that their marriage would be a great testimony of God's faithfulness, love and mercy as their light shines to the world around them.

PRONOUNCEMENT AS HUSBAND AND WIFE - The pronouncement officially declares that the bride and groom are now husband and wife. This is welcome with ecstasy by the congregation, there is shout of alleluia and clapping of hands. The couple are happy and fulfilled, the congregation shares in their joy. This moment establishes the precise beginning of their marriage covenant. The two are now one in the eyes of God and human beings.

PRESENTATION OF THE COUPLE - When the minister introduces the couple to the wedding guests, he is drawing attention to their new identity, and the change of name brought about by their marriage. They are now Mr. and Mrs. so…so…so… taking the family name of the husband. Their status has changed to a higher level.

SIGNING AND PRESENTATION OF MARRIAGE CERTIFICATE: With joy in hearts and dancing, the newlyweds proceed to sign their marriage certificate in the place earmarked for the occasion. The congregation remains in the church with music and dancing. This is the final seal on the joining of this husband and wife. The couple will sign, parents, officiating ministers and some other chosen persons given the honour will sign as well. They sign to testify that they are witnesses to the joining of the two in marriage. The couple returns to the congregation dancing and singing and the pastor who joined them will present the certificate to the couple before the congregation.

PRAYERS FOR THE COUPLE – As husband and wife. Special prayers are said for this newlyweds as they commence their marital journey, just as it was said by God in Eden to the first couple – Adam and Eve in Genesis 1:28 – to be fruitful and multiply, to replenish the earth and subdue it and to have dominion over all.

ANNOUNCEMENT- Thanksgiving on behalf of the couple to all guests and participants. The reception follows immediately after. Some photographs could be taken inside and outside the church, most importantly the newlyweds and the officiating ministers.

THROWING OF CONFETTI – Confetti are small, colourful pieces of papers or metallic materials which are usually thrown at celebrations, most especially at weddings. It is always done as the couple emerges from the church and also as they enter the reception with dances. It is a festive token to add glamor. It is a way of saying "Congratulations" to the new couple. Confetti also symbolizes the future fertility and prosperity of the couple.

Source

THE RECEPTION – This is their first social appearance as husband and wife after the wedding. A ceremonial meal was often part of the blood covenant in the Old Testament as well as in the New Testament. For example Jesus instituted the Holy Communion also known as the Lord's Supper as the meal of the New Testament with in His blood in I Corinthians 11:24-25. At a wedding reception, guests share with the couple in the abundant blessings of their marriage covenant, eating and drinking in celebration. The reception also illustrates the wedding supper of the Lamb described in Revelation 19: 17 -21.

ENTRANCE OF LATEST COUPLE WITH DANCE – A sign of gratitude to God, achievement and fulfilment of their marriage ceremony. They glorify God in their dances for making their wedding a reality. This is done in different styles, also with pomp and pageantry, all glory must be to the Lord.

WEDDING CAKE - CUTTING AND FEEDING OF CAKE - The wedding cake symbolizes good fortune and fertility. It also brings good wishes to everyone who eats it. The wedding cake should be made with an abundance of good quality ingredients to symbolize a long-lasting, rich, and happy marriage. The bride and groom cut the cake and feed each other with the first slice to show how they will share their good life and fortune together, taking care of each other. In Nigeria, and in the commonwealth, well preserved cakes used to last longer so as to parcel it to relatives overseas.

When the bride and groom take pieces of cake and feed it to each other, once again, they are showing they have given their all to the other and will care for each other as one flesh. At a Christian wedding, the cutting and feeding of cake is done with style. Often the baker is around to present the cake. He or she will tell about the significances of the ingredients used and colors in which the cake is decorated before the cutting. The cutting and feeding each other with cake is done lovingly and reverently, in a way that honors the covenant relationship

TOAST TO THE BRIDE AND GROOM & RESPONSE - This is a social recognition of the groom and bride as a couple and to wish them the best in their union. A little may be said about how they came to know or meet each other by the best man, a close friend or anyone who knows much about them. Guests will rise and click glasses to toast with non-alcoholic wine or water to wish the newlyweds the best.   Couple would dance together with parents and others after the toast.

PRESENTATION OF GIFTS – a symbol of happiness and well wishes for the couple. The gifts should not be received directly by the couple, someone else should arrange for how to receive the gifts and how the gifts will get to the couple latter. Prayers should be said on the gifts to counteract any evil machinations of the enemy.

VOTES OF THANKS, CLOSING PRAYERS AND BENEDICTION - signifies the end of the wedding ceremonies. After this the couple goes on their honey moon.

Truly, the Christian wedding is rich with meaningful actions and symbolisms. If a couple understands the meaning and significance of all these symbols, and if taken to heart, by the couples, it will guide them and secure them as they tread the long and winding road called marriage with fear and trembling. Every bride and groom -to -be, looking forward to this royal event should please run away from fornication. No fornicator would have the grace to enjoy being celebrated in a marriage like this. Keep yourself pure. Be wise.

WEDDING SYMBOLS

QUESTION 53

IF MARRIAGE VOWS ARE BIDING WHY DO WE HAVE PEOPLE DUMPING, SEPARATING, AND SOME DIVORCING THEIR SPOUSES,

EVEN IN THE CHURCH TODAY?

The Pharisees asked Jesus this same question in Mathew 19: 3"Is it lawful for a man to put away his wife for every cause?

Jesus answered saying unto them," have ye not read, that he which made them at the beginning made them male and female…Wherefore they are no more two, but one flesh. What therefore God has joined together, let not man put asunder."

The Pharisees pressed further to query why Moses permitted husbands to put away their wives in the days of Moses? "He said unto them, Moses because of the hardness of your hearts suffered you to put away your wives; but from the beginning it was not so" Jesus was referring to the beginning of creation - of the woman from man; and the institution marriage as planned and ordained by God in Genesis 2:18- 25.

As it was in the days of Moses, so it is now. The hearts of some husbands and wives are hard, stony and very wicked, and only God knows! - The heart is deceitful above all things, and desperately wicked: who can know it? Jeremiah 17:9 Men who profess to be Christian are now putting away their wives for whatever reasons. This is treachery and blatant disobedience to the will of God Who wants marriage to be a life-time relationship.

These men and women are usually offensive, hard hearted, selfish and unfaithful to their marital vows. They will always have some excuse to defend their doings, which shows that their own lewd imaginations have deceived them and brought them so low, that they finally opted for divorce. But God will examine their wicked deeds by the malice of their hearts bring them to book. Jesus says it is impossible for husbands and wives not to offend each other, there will be sure ground for divorce like adultery, separation and abandonment. "… but woe unto him, though whom they come-Luke 17:1.

After saying "I do" and "Till death do us part" - Whatever the situation, no matter the magnitude of the offence, we are told to forgive! Because of the hardness of their heart men and women have chosen to forgive. Forgiveness generally is defined as a conscious, deliberate decision to release feelings of resentment or vengeance towards a person who has offended you or harm you, regardless of whatever they have done. Forgiveness does not mean excusing nor condoning offenses. It is saying you deserved to be punished for what you have done, but I am not going to punish you for the sake of the vows I have made to you and because of my love for and obedience to God – Malachi 2: 14 -16.

"Yet ye say, wherefore? Because the LORD hath been witness between thee and the wife of thy youth, against whom thou hast dealt treacherously: yet is she thy companion, and the wife of thy covenant. And did not he make one? Yet had he the residue of the spirit. And wherefore one? That he might seek a godly seed. Therefore take heed to your spirit, and let none deal treacherously against the wife of his youth. For the LORD, the God of Israel, saith that he hateth putting away: for one covereth violence with his garment, saith the LORD of hosts: therefore take heed to your spirit that ye deal not treacherously".

Forgiveness is for the happiness and peace of the people offended. When you hold on to hurt, anger, bitterness, pain, disappointment and resentment, it harms you more than the offender. "To err is human and to forgive divine". There is no perfect human relationship yet because every one of us – men and women are still working towards perfection, we are all flawed human beings prone to make mistakes – big and small. Forgiveness frees you from the bondage of the past, and allows you to enjoy the beauty of the present.

"Brethren, I count not myself to have apprehended: but this one thing I do, forgetting those things which are behind, and reaching forth unto those things which are before," I press toward the mark for the prize of the high calling of God in Christ Jesus. 15Let us therefore, as many as be perfect, be thus minded: and if in anything ye be otherwise minded, God shall reveal even this unto you. Nevertheless, whereto we have already attained, let us walk by the same rule, let us mind the same thing".

In the Marriage dictionary of God, we have confession, repentance, acceptance , unconditional love, longsuffering, forgiveness, and every other word that will contribute to making marriage a heaven on earth relationship and that will make husband and wife stay together through thick and thin, till death do them part. The only word that cannot be found in the marriage dictionary of God is "DIVORCE". Divorce implies double voice – double tongue; you have said "Yes I do" you cannot say "No I don't" anymore. God hates divorce, He does not like men to put away or divorce their wives for any reason.

Whether you like it or not, divorce is from the pit of hell. Anybody who is contemplating on putting away his wife or husband is being hardhearted and stubborn, and should desist from it. Anyway, you can choose to do whatever you like after all the persuasions and begging; but you cannot choose the consequences of your act of disobedience to God and mankind. If you sow to the flesh, you are sure bound to reap corruption.

It is written-

"He, that being often reproved hardeneth his neck, shall suddenly be destroyed, and that without remedy" .Proverbs 29:1.

QUESTION 54
CAN A PASTOR WHO DIVORCED HIS WIFE REMARRY ANOTHER WIFE?

The answer is Capital NO!

There are pastors and there are pastors! A pastor is supposed to be a man of God, a shepherd, a care taker and a role model for the church members. He is to be exemplary in all. Honestly, such a pastor has missed it. The world may accept it, tradition may favor it and socio- cultural environment may codon it, in any case, it is an error. In divorce, you are not only disobeying God, you are acting God – you are on your own! You are in the flesh, manifesting the spirit of anger, bitterness, resentment and unforgiveness. In your anger you have no regard for the law of God concerning marriage. You have avenged yourself on your spouse, that is why you sent her away, but God says vengeance belongs to him.

God says –"I hate divorce", He calls is treachery. It is a gross disobedience to God, and a violation of divine rights of the founder of marriage – For the LORD, the God of Israel, saith that he hateth putting away: for one covereth violence with his garment, saith the LORD of hosts: therefore take heed to your spirit that ye deal not treacherously". Malachi 2: 16.

In the first instance, it is wrong for anyone professing Christian talk less of a Pastor to be divorced. For your information divorce has never and can never be a solution. Divorce is for escapists- those who are running away from the realities of life. No man or woman is perfect, perfect marriages are still under construction. It takes two to tango – no spouse can ever be innocent in a marital conflict. The law of harvest cannot be faulted – whatever you sow you will surely reap. Love will always beget love and in hatred, if your mother is onion and your father is garlic you have to option but to smell.

Before you divorce, you ought to have gone down the memory lane, think of what brought you together. How did you meet? What did you see in each other before you said "Yes I do" in the presence of God and holy witnesses who heard you made your vows. Whatever has happened between then and now that you have decided to run away from your God - given responsibilities in marriage is not of God, it is from the pit of hell. It is nothing but a satanic agenda to discredit you and to stop you from fulfilling the plan and purposes of God, not only for you but for your wife, children and those around you.

Secondly, as a Pastor, who are you representing? You cannot be a servant of the Most High God and choose to do what he does not like. What lessons are you teaching the members of your church? In your disobedience you are going to drag many of your followers to hell. You are telling them you can avenge yourself, do what you like, when you like it and how you like it- no matter what the Word of God says about it!. They would think it is right to send a wife packing and just take on another one! – Just like you change clothes? NO sir. You have violated the Christian Constitutional right of "One man, and one woman in the Lord" You need to wake up from your backsliding and run back to God in repentance.

Thirdly, you have no right to go on violating the act of marriage by looking for another person to deceive. You lied to the first woman that you loved her, whereas you did not. If your love for her had been genuine, it should have been strong enough to pardon her, spare her head in marriage and continue to love her unconditionally.   It is whoremongers that jump from one woman without any shame to another one – you are not a butterfly pollinating about, you are polluting. Now, are you so sure that the new wife you have taken would not offend you? She might even do worse things. Will you send her packing like the first one too? You see the futility of divorce – it is running from frying pan into fire. It does not solve any problem it only complicates life and compound problems.

God is not a God of confusion. Once you are divorced you are saying marriage is too hard, you cannot continue, then stop marrying. You cannot marry again. Since you cannot live any longer with your first wife with all the disappointments, dissatisfactions and unhappiness, the best thing for you is to remain single. Marriage is not a life of game or chance, it is a life of commitment, endurance and adaptation in obedience to God. You are permitted to repent and go back to your first love. You cannot take on any other wife in error.

Finally, It is written – "Whosoever shall put away his wife except it be for fornication and shall marry another, committed adultery: and whoso marrieth her which is put away doth commit adultery" Mathew 19:9.

According to the word of God such a pastor is an adulterer, the woman he is planning to marry is also and adulteress. Marriage is honorable and the marital bed must remain sanctified. God will judge Adulterers, fornicators and whoremongers. None of them will go to heaven, unless they repent- Rev. 21:8.

So therefore, neither a man nor a woman who had been married before and for whatsoever reason divorced is permitted to marry. Be reconciled or stay single till death takes you away.

QUESTION 55
WHY IS THE CHRISTIAN MARRIAGE INDISSOLUBLE?

The Christian marriage is indissoluble because God who ordained it has said so. Marriage is life – bound. Only death can separate a wedded husband and wife. Nothing is allowed to separate the man and woman joined in holy matrimony in the presence of God and people witnessing. That is how God wants it, and that settles it. Jesus Christ also reiterated the permanency of marriage when He was answering the question of the Pharisees who said Moses allowed divorce among the Israelites during their wilderness experience -

"But from the beginning of the creation God made them male and female.

For this cause shall a man leave his father and mother, and cleave to his wife; And they twain shall be one flesh: so then they are no more twain,

but one flesh. What therefore God hath joined together, let not man put asunder". "Mark 10: 6-9

What is marriage? Simply put, it is the union of one man and one woman in the Lord.

"Therefore a man shall leave his father and his mother and hold fast to his wife, and they shall become one flesh". Genesis 2:24

In Malachi 2:14, marriage is described as a holy covenant before God. One of the reasons why we celebrate marriage as a ceremony in the church is so that in the presence of God the creator of the man and the woman; and before a Holy Congregation who serve as a witness, the two will exchange their vows. So the vows, signing of marriage certificate are meant to be a public demonstration of a couple's acceptance and preparedness to enter into the covenant of marriage for life as ordained by God. It is not the ceremony that is very important but the couple's covenant commitment before God and the people of God.

We can see clearly that marriage is not a product of human imagination or social evolution. Marriage came down from God, He has the right to tell us how to do it, because it belongs to him. It is very sad that divorce and remarriage are very common today and practiced even in the church. God says marriage is indissoluble, He does not want divorce. Marriage is a covenant agreement, meant for life, therefore it must not be broken under any circumstance; remarriage further violates the covenant and therefore is not permissible.

QUESTION 56

APART FROM BEING AN ACT OF DISOBEDIENCE TO GOD, ARE THERE OTHER REASONS WHY DIVORCE SHOULD NOT BE PERMITTED?

Divorce, also known as dissolution of marriage, is the process of terminating a marriage or marital union by a court or other competent body. Divorce is against the plan and purpose of God for marriage. In the Christian marriage there should be no divorce, and no remarriage. Divorce is an aberration and we know it does not really solve any problem, it rather complicates the lives of the divorcees.

Prevention is always better than cure. People planning to marry should be made to understand and accept marriage as a lifelong relationship before taking the vows before God and men.

If you got married, you promised to stay married forever. That was for richer or poorer (through the financial difficulties), in sickness and in health (even when illness disrupts your life and causes emotional turmoil), for better or worse (through all the problems and all the successes of life). On that wedding day, you promised that you would love, cherish and obey; that you would be there for each other, no matter what. These words are binding. You are obliged to be a man and woman of your words till you die. Nothing on earth should ever be allowed to separate those that God has joined together in marriage. The unconditional love of God makes all things to work together for good for husbands and wives. They are always more than conquerors through Christ. It is written:-

"Who shall separate us from the love of Christ? Shall tribulation, or persecution, or famine, or nakedness or peril, or sword? ,,,For I am persuaded that neither death nor life, nor angels, nor principalities , no powers, nor things present, nor things to come, nor height nor death, nor any other creature, shall be able to separate us from the love of God, which is in Christ Jesus our Lord. Nay in all these things, we are more than conquerors through him that loved us" Amen.

In reality, divorce and remarriage is becoming a norm in these last days. The love of self, headiness or hard heartedness, and blatant disobedience to God are the manifestation of end time events – This know also, that in the last days perilous times shall come. For men shall be lovers of their own selves, covetous, boasters, proud, blasphemers, disobedient to parents, unthankful, unholy, Without natural affection, trucebreakers, false accusers, incontinent, fierce, despisers of those that are good, Traitors, heady, high-minded, lovers of pleasures more than lovers of God; Having a form of godliness, but denying the power thereof: from such turn away.

Run away from divorce because of the evil effects or consequences of it. Divorce should not be permitted, it should be avoided like Corona virus by all means because of the following:-

Marriage makes a man and a woman one flesh, with complete union of body, soul and spirit, union of interests, fortunes, desires, sorrows and joys – how do you separate all these in a divorce?

Please try this God-given and Holy Spirit inspired illustration - to show that divorce is ugly, and no one can ever stay clean and clear from a divorce after. Draw two images of a husband and wife on two papers, of different colors – representing husband and wife. Cut out the shapes and glue them together to make one paper. - representing their coming together as husband and wife, becoming one entity on their wedding day, the glue represents the vows and the certificate of marriage they made, signed and received on their wedding day. Leave the joined colored papers out to dry. You can drop any dirt, liquid, food particles, stamp on it –representing the problems and challenges of life. The glued paper remains one though dirty and roughened by life challenges. As long as they remain one, husband and wife will be able to absorb and get over whatever is trying to soil their marital relationship.

On the other hand, if they allow the problems to soil and tear them apart in divorce, they will be too bartered to be recognized. Now, try and separate the glued papers that have become one. The picture of what you get will be pitiable. If you have used two colours – Green and white, by the time you tear them up, it will neither be green not white. It will be tattered and ugly to behold. That is what divorce does to a husband and wife. When you want to separate what God has joined together you end up frustrated, marred and too shattered to be whole gain. DIVORCE IS A POISON, PLEASE DON'T TAKE IT.

The evil consequences on their children and other family members. Husband and wives should please stay married because of their children they have produced out of love. Children will never get over the loss of their family and their lives will never be the same. There will be long-lasting spiritual, emotional, financial, physical developmental, academic, moral and psychological repercussions on those children. Their lives or destiny may be truncated because of the error of the parents who brought them into the world. What a pity?

Divorce causes emotional devastation for husband and wife – Though they may deny it and put on bold face, there is always pain with separation. A French writer Andre Malraux says –"separation is a kind of death". All the hopes, dreams of living together, holding hands till when old and feeble are shattered. Divorce is a type of death and we will need to grieve the loss of the relationship just as we would if a person we love died. The worst thing is the man or woman is still alive, not dead but lost in the world. People say that the death of a child is better than sudden disappearance of the child. Divorce is a sudden disappearance of someone who should be with you for life, it is painful.

Loss of Identity – With divorce your status will change for worse. When divorce occurs, husband and wife lose that marital role of husband or wife. You are no longer the husband or wife of so- and- so. You are now an EX- not a good title, it is degrading. Women feel this in a very literal way as they go from "Mrs." to a "Ms." Not only that, many women are forced to change their name back to their maiden name as they don't want to continue to identify with a name that no longer reflects who they are. Some women may actually breakdown mentally, and some have died suddenly - emotionally wrecked. Because marriage gives us a strong identity and role in this world, and divorce takes that away.

Financial struggles and added expenses - The longer a couple stays married, the more time they have to build assets. Divorce disrupts building of assets, birth liabilities and forces both husband and wife to start from scratch. In divorce you have to pay for two homes instead of one, you run more, you are unstable – neither here nor there. Now, one person usually the woman must find a way to care for the children because most of the time the man does not look back and cares less about mother and children in the developing societies. In developed societies the man must a pay large amount of money to help her do this. Economically, this is far harder than doing it together. Both parties lose in a child support situation. Before you divorce, be sure to consider the consequences, because they are serious.

Loneliness and loss of social even spiritual circles – Marriage was designed for companionship, friendship, fellowship and intimacy. Husband and wife who once have enjoyed it find it very hard and difficult to live alone in divorce. Divorce has a dramatic effect on your social circle- you are neither here nor there. A person's marital status is important and affects the dynamics of most social interactions. Couples often feel more comfortable being with other couples. Some couples don't feel comfortable around a divorced person and prefers to avoid such socially.

A divorced minister has to be ministered to first and foremost, what do you have to give? You are in disobedience. Because the church will not want others to follow your example, you are left alone to repent and go back to your first love.

Stigmatization - "You are a divorcee" "Divorcees are not allowed to…" Most especially in spiritual circles and social gatherings where divorce is permitted but not really allowed. Anybody who has studied or witnessed the aftermath of divorced know it is a tragic mistake, and they want you to stay together with your spouse and resolve your problems together.

Divorce strikes a heavy blow at everyone involved, even those who are involved peripherally, like teachers, friends, and society in general. The suffering from divorce will happen, and nobody wants you to go through with it. No one really benefits from divorce except lawyers and therapists who may usually make money out of it. The current generation minimizes the consequences of divorce. It even venerates it! What a pity!

QUESTION 57
WHAT ARE BIBLICAL REASONS OR GROUNDS FOR DIVORCE?

The Bible is God's inspired revelation of the origin and destiny of all things, written in thousands of simple human languages possible, so that everybody can understand and obey its teaching. The Bible reveals the mind of God and it covers every subject of human knowledge and affairs, applicable now and forever. The doctrines of the Bible are holy, its precepts biding, its histories are true and its decisions unchangeable. We have to study it, read it to be wise, believe it to be safe, commit it to memory and practice it to be holy. 2 Timothy 3: 16 -17; 2 Peter 1:21.

The Bible speaks on divorce in many places at different times. Permission to divorce was granted by Moses under the dispensation of Law during the wilderness experience of the Israelites. Divorce was granted because of the hardness of the hearts of the people. The whole discourse is brought out clearly in the gospel according to Saint Matthew, chapter 19: 3 – 9.

"The Pharisees also came unto him, tempting him, and saying unto him, Is it lawful for a man to put away his wife for every cause?4 And he answered and said unto them, Have ye not read, that he which made them at the beginning made them male and female, And said, for this cause shall a man leave father and mother, and shall cleave to his wife: and they twain shall be one flesh?6 Wherefore they are no more twain, but one flesh. What therefore God hath joined together, let not man put asunder.7 They say unto him, why did Moses then command to give a writing of divorcement, and to put her away?8 He saith unto them, Moses because of the hardness of your hearts suffered you to put away your wives: but from the beginning it was not so.9 And I say unto you, whosoever shall put away his wife, except it be for fornication, and shall marry another, committeth adultery: and whoso marrieth her which is put away doth commit adultery".

The word of God is truth and the Bible does not contradict itself. In the New Testament period of grace, divorce is allowed on the ground of adultery or marital unfaithfulness. People have interpreted marital unfaithfulness in many different ways in the church. The sin of fornication or adultery found in Matthew 19:9 - can be any form of sexual immorality including adultery, prostitution, fornication, pornography, and incest. Since sexual union is such a crucial part of the marriage covenant, breaking that bond seems to be a permissible, biblical grounds for divorce.

However, Jesus through His death and resurrection has reestablished the permanency of marriage as ordained by God when He commanded us to forgive those who sinned against us. No man or woman should divorce the spouse because of the sin of adultery or fornication. A perfect marriage is just two imperfect people who refuse to give up on each other. The truth of the Bible must be divided dispensational, prophetically, historically and with regard for classes and subjects. We should gather from the Scriptures themselves the precise meaning the writer intended to convey. Not only to get the true meaning, but also the true application to the various times and classes of people. In this dispensation of grace, the Christian marriage in the church of God is to be received as a life-bound relationship, only physical death- the end of life can put an end to marriage.

If any of the spouses got involved in marital unfaithfulness, the culprit must be confronted. Whoever breaks the vows by having affairs outside marriage is in a backsliding state – is dead spiritually- being separated from God, such should just confess, repent, forsake the evil way and return back to God. Proverbs 28:13 "He that covereth his transgressions shall not prosper; but whoso confesseth and forsaketh them shall obtain mercy". If any husband and wife wants to live long and finish strong martially, they must forgive one another just as the lord has forgiven them- Colossians 3:13.

As far as Jesus is concerned, divorce is not the solution for marital unfaithfulness but forgiveness; there is always room for reconciliation. When sin is confronted, confessed and forsaken, the other spouse should forgive. God does not want the death of a sinner, he or she should confess and forsake them to have mercy of God and people. The other spouse should learn to forgive. Remember the story of the wicked, according to Mathew 18: 32 -35.

Anyone who indulges himself in sexual sin should be exposed and disciplined. Such a person may be suspended from ministering in the church for a period of time and then reinstated after the punishment. Church discipline should always apply when someone sins against God. "Moreover if your brother sins against you, go and tell him his fault between you and him alone. If he hears you, you have gained your brother." Mt 18:15. It may be hard, a spouse involved in adultery should not only confess to God, but must confess to the cheated spouse too. When true confession is made, the offended spouse should forgive. By the grace of God forgiveness is better than disregarding the marriage vows and entering into a life of defeat and shame in divorce.

The importance of forgiveness in the place of divorce when there is sin of adultery cannot be overemphasized – "The Peter came up and said to him, "Lord, how often will my brother sin against me, and 1 forgive him? As many as seven times?" Jesus said to him, "I do not say to you seven times, but seventy times seven times. Mathew 18: 21-22. Jesus encourages all believers to forgive and receive forgiveness times without number. Seventy signifies spiritual perfection. Seventy times seven means we need to forgive someone completely, and not let it continue to fester or play over again and again in our minds. Jesus teaches us to be forgiving, not just for the other person's sake but for the forgiveness we too have received from God through Christ Jesus.

When we are saved, and become born again by grace through faith in Christ Jesus, the unconditional – Agape love of God that enables us to love and forgive is shed abroad in our regenerated hearts. God's love manifested through the cross transforms our minds, hearts, will, and life such that we become aligned with God's will and purposes in marriage. "And God is able to make all grace abound to you, that ye always having sufficiency in all things, may abound to every good work" 2 Corinthians 9:8. Forgiveness is an act of grace. God is glorified and highly honored in marriage by those who forgive others.

In these last days, the devil is out to destroy homes and scatter families. Many unbelievable and unimaginable sins are being committed today in the family. A lot of abuse are happening in the family between husband and wives, parents and children, children and other members of the family. If a spouse becomes dangerous, abusive or addicted to a substance or has abandoned the family out rightly, there may be a need for a breathing space of separation to safe life. You must continue to pray and go for counseling for these problems to be solved. Please don't pack out of your matrimonial home. God, the creator of all flesh is the one who started marriage. Nothing is too difficult for you. He will make a way out of these problems for you. With God all things are possible.

In other words, if your spouse is verbally, physically or psychologically abusing you - beating and slapping you at the least provocation, you need to speak to your pastor. If the spouse is an alcoholic or a drug addict, has dumped you and finally left you for someone else, some secular family therapists say you can divorce, but l will say that is not the will of God for you. If you are living in any of these conditions, and you are thinking of getting a divorce, please wait a little and consider the evil consequences of divorce. Instead of divorce, I suggest you talk to your pastor and seek advice from your counselling department. Pray, fast and cry out to God, God will hear your voice, He will help you and your problems will become testimonies in the name of Jesus. "…call on me in the day of trouble: I will deliver you, and you shall glorify me". Psalm 15:5.

QUESTION 58

MY SPOUSE SAYS "I WANT A DIVORCE" WHAT SHOULD I DO?

It is a reality of life that the only permanent thing in life is change. Time changes, seasons change, cultural value changes and people change as well. What on earth could have caused somebody who said "I do" sometimes ago, to change his mind and say "I want a divorce?" only God knows the heart of man. You know, we are in the last days, perilous time has come and the unthinkable are happening. Whatever the situation, I want you to encourage yourself in the Lord, trust in His word and obey Him. If you will be willing and obedient to godly counsel, even if you have made mistakes, God will have mercy, He will arise and fight for you and save your marriage from this satanic assault, in the name of Jesus. Amen.

"There hath no temptation taken you but such as is common to man:

but God is faithful, who will not suffer you to be tempted above that ye are able; but will with the temptation also make a way to escape,

that ye may be able to bear it". 1 Corinthians 10:13

Reconciliation of a husband and wife is easier if one of them does not want the dissolution of the marriage. The one who believes in the union no matter what may have happened should stand up and fight for the marriage. God is the creator of marriage, He is the God of all flesh and with Him nothing shall be impossible.

Trust in the LORD, and do good; so shalt thou dwell in the land,

and verily thou shalt be fed. Delight thyself also in the LORD;

and he shall give thee the desires of thine heart. Commit thy way unto the LORD; trust also in him; and he shall bring it to pass.

Therefore, stand up for your marriage and prayerfully with faith in God, do the following:

Be calm, do not entertain fear and don't be discouraged. Like David in the book of Samuel 30:6 - encourage yourself in the Lord your God. All of us one time or the other face a crisis when everything seems to fall apart. There are times of discouragement, when things go wrong even when we are trying to do right. David needed to, and so will you. If he could do it to recover all, you can also do it to safe your marriage.

Take a personal inventory and search your heart - Ask yourself "In what way have I contributed to this?" - Is it in my Anger, too much resentment, unforgiveness, bitterness, selfishness, self-centeredness? Cheating or adultery? Emotional black out? Loneliness? Lack of love, disrespect, ignoring and avoiding your spouse?

It takes two to tango, no spouse can really be innocent in a situation like this. Your ignorance or carelessness may have led to this. In any case, ask God to help you, to open your eyes to see your own flaws. Understand how your behavior has affected your spouse and caused him or her to want a divorce.

Meanwhile, call your pastor and inform him about the situation, don't engage in arguments and don't begin to rain abuse or blame shift. Let God have his way in this matter. Your own good has not been too good for your relationship. You have to begin to do something better, behave well and change your attitude to determine your altitude. The Lord will lift you up, in the name of Jesus.

Do not pack out of your matrimonial home. Don't give any chance to the devil. Stop doing things that will make the situation worse – fighting, nagging, stop being critical and complaining, stop blowing up and losing your temper, put your focus on saving the marriage not on who is at fault. Two wrongs can never make a right. You must be looking for solution, the way out of this problem.

Humble yourself, resist pride - for 'God resists the proud, but gives grace to the humble.' Pride goes before a fall. Humble yourselves therefore under the mighty hand of God, that he may exalt you in due time; 1 Peter 5:6. Humbly ask your spouse to forgive you, be patient with you, give you time to discuss the reason(s) why this is happening to both of you, and why you cannot be divorced. You have to work out together the way forward. Divorce is never a solution to marital problems.

Counseling is cheaper than divorce. Go for counseling with or without your spouse first – find out why and how the situation can be resolved without a divorce. Work on how to safe your marriage. Divorce complicates and disrupts life, your life can never be the same again after a divorce. Act with wisdom. Stop being pettily reactive and start healing your marital relationship. No blaming, no excuses for the past (apologies are acceptable), and get to work.

Engage is warfare and deliverance prayers for your family – Have faith in God. Settle this assault from the pit of hell spiritually and prayerfully. God is for you, Jesus has defeated principalities and powers, household wickedness, envious and jealous people, anti-marriage ancestral spirits and all sorts of witchcraft manipulations on the cross. He has made a public show of them on the cross, triumphing over them. You are more than conquerors through Christ. Your reconciliation will manifest, God will touch the heart of your spouse, and there shall be reconciliation.

I have good news for you, we can stop divorce. When couples decide to work on their marriages, it does not matters who is at fault, they always win! Such couples eventually come around, blind eyes are opened, hard hearts are softened, sometimes it takes a bit, but reconciliation surely comes to pass to the glory of God and the shame of the devil. SO DON'T GIVE UP! STAND UP FOR YOUR MARIAGE, AND LET THERE BE RECONCILIATION. It is never too late to stop any divorce process. Don't lose the best friend you have ever had because of a few minor or major problems.

Divorce is destroying our nations, societies and eroding families. The family is the bedrock of all human societies. The state of the family is reflected in the state of the nations. Stable families make up stable societies and nations at large. As Christians it should be our passion and mission to prevent, avoid and stop divorce. Churches should now made it their life's mission to eradicate the need for divorce through marriage education. We must do everything we can to combat the causes of divorce at every level through sound biblical doctrinal teachings. No true child or minister of God should ever indulge in divorce. God says I hate divorce, it is high time we begin to honor and respect the God we profess to know and serve by doing only His will in marriage. May the Lord help us in the name of Jesus. Amen.

SETTLEMENT IN MARRIAGE

QUESTION 59

MY HUSBAND SNORES TOO MUCH AND IT KEEPS ME AWAKE ALMOST ALL THE NIGHT, WHAT CAN WE DO?

You are welcome to the group of the married. One of the things you may not know about your spouse during courtship is that he or she snores. Snoring once in a while is not a serious problem, nearly everyone does that. However, for some people it can be a chronic health challenge and it could be disturbing to the other partner. Snoring is the hoarse or harsh sound that occurs when air flows past relaxed tissues in the throat, causing the tissues to vibrate as one breathes.

For those concerned, you snore because your breathing is obstructed in some way, usually because relaxed tissue is blocking your airway. As you breathe in, the air flowing past these tissues causes them to vibrate, and that vibration is what causes the sound you make when you snore. It is may be irritating for the other partner in bed. The vibrations are caused by turbulent airflow through narrowed airways. Snoring is enhanced by Nasal congestion, sleep position or posture, excess weight, sleeping with an open mouth, allergies and aging.

Since what is causing the obstruction can differ from one snorer to the other, you need to see a doctor and find out exactly what is causing that obstruction in your spouse and seek remedy accordingly.

Sometimes snoring may also indicate a serious health issue most especially for those who take alcohol or smoke. Alcohol and smoking may depress the central nervous system and causes the throat muscle to relax, in other words the vibrations could be more turbulent. Lifestyle changes, such as losing weight, avoiding alcohol, not smoking, and taking the right posture when sleeping will put an end to snoring. As you work together to find solution to this problem, pray that the love of God – Agape will continue to knit your hearts together in your relationship, in the name of Jesus.

MARRIAGE RELATIONSHIP, ROLES AND DUTIES

QUESTION 60

HOW CAN WE MAKE A SUCCESS OF OUR MARRIAGE?

"As ye have therefore received Christ Jesus the Lord, so walk ye in him, rooted and built up in Him, and stablished in the faith as ye have been taught, abounding therein with thanksgiving" Colossians 2:8-7

As you have started your relationship with the love of God through Jesus Christ, continue like that, looking unto Jesus the author and beginning of your marriage. Be guided by the word of God in faith as you have been taught in premarital counseling. Continue to love each other, accept each other, and appreciate each other. Let the word of God guide you in all matters and obey the rules of God concerning marriage at all times. Pray always pray, committing yourselves and your relationship to God, let the Holy Spirit lead and guide you in all. If you are willing to obey God in all things, you will make a success of your marriage.

"This book of law shall not depart out of thy mouth, but thou shalt meditate therein day and night that thou mayest observe to do according to all that, for then thou shalt make thy way prosperous,

and then thou shalt have good success" Joshua 1:8.

QUESTION 61

WHAT ARE THE IMPLICATIONS OF HUSBAND BEIGN THE

HEAD OF THE FAMILY?

The position of the husband as the head of the family is divinely appointed. Just as Christ is the Head of the Catholic Church (the family of God), so the father is the head of his domestic church (his family) - "But I want you to understand that the head of every man is Christ, the head of a woman is her husband, and the head of Christ is God." 1 Cor. 11:3

The man was the first to be created, and the woman out of him and was made for him. Therefore the man has precedence. He is first in order and must be the head and chief priest of the family. Headship is a position of authority, the husband is the governor, director, administrator, the captain, the general overseer and the commander in chief of the family.

The husband as a head coordinates the affairs of the family. He has authority over his wife and children. His exemplary, Christ like leadership at home command the submission, cooperation, respect and followership of the wife and children. The husband should endeavor to live up to this exalted position as the head of the family. He has an example to follow in Jesus Christ.

We have a manifestation of headship demonstrated for us in history. Jesus, the Son of God, equal to the Father in his deity, nevertheless, when he assumes humanity, submits himself to the leadership of the Father. Everywhere Jesus went he stated this. "I do always those things which please my Father." On one occasion he said, "My meat is to do my Father's will, and to please him who sent me…John 4:34. As Christ is the head of the church and the church is subject to Him, so the husband is the head of the wife, and she is to be subject to the husband in everything. The wife should always do the will of the husband and endeavor to please him in all things.

Moreover, the man as the head of the woman is to provide and care for her, to nourish and cherish her, to protect and defend her against all insults and injuries.

QUESTION 62

WHAT ARE THE RESPONSIBILITIES OF A HUSBAND?

All of a husband's duties can be summed up in one simple command-

"Husbands, love your wives, even as Christ also loved the Church,

and gave himself for her" Ephes. 5:25.

The husband's duty to his wife is enforced by a type, a simile - it should correspond to Christ's love for the Church, and should be comparable to the love the husband has for himself - "So ought men to love their wives as their own bodies,

He that loveth his wife loveth himself?

For no man ever yet hated his own flesh; but nourisheth and cherisheth it,

even as the Lord the church". Ephes 5: 28-29.

A husband should care deeply for his wife whom the Lord has given him. There is nothing that she wants more from her marriage than to know that she is loved and cherished. Honestly, few things are worse and sadder than an unloved wife. The husband who initiates in love will help his wife to respond in greater love and respect for him.

A husband ought to love the wife sacrificially and unconditionally just as Jesus Christ loved the church and gave his life for her. The love must be a purifying love so that the wife will be more spiritual, spotless, holy and more beautiful within and without than when she left her father and mother and was joined to you in marriage.

A husband should love his wife as dearly as he loves himself. A husband should spare no effort in caring for his one and only wife. As it is unnatural for a man to abuse his own body, it is also unnatural and self- destructive for a man to neglect or mistreat his wife.

A wife needs far more than material nourishment. It is the sole responsibility of the husband to meet her emotional needs as well. A husband should love his wife with an understanding love, and show her honor as a fellow heir of the grace of life so that his prayers will not be hindered –I Peter 3:7. A husband who loves his wife will know what brings her joy. He will seek to understand what their sexual union means to her and will seek to serve her in that area unreservedly.

Finally, a husband should treat his wife with respect, recognize her God – given role as a helper needed and designed for him, listen to her attentively, and seek her opinion in family matters. Do not micromanage your wife, give her freedom in her realms of life as a woman, just as the husband in Proverbs 31 trusts the virtuous woman to run the household home economics profitably, demonstrating her Gog- given initiatives and business acumen.

Unfortunately, many husbands are authoritarians, offensive and very critical. They manage their homes by belittling and limiting their wives, ignoring what is done right, while carefully pointing out the ways their wives fall short of their expectations. Negativism, constant criticism is like a cancer that eats away the heart of a marriage. Your wife is not perfect, but neither are you.

A husband who selfishly exercises dominion in his marriage, expecting everything to revolve around him from how the money is spent to what the family eats on the table does not know how to love. Such ought to cry out to God for divine intervention and trust in God for help. It is written- "And such trust have we through Christ to God – ward;

Not that we are sufficient of ourselves to think anything as of ourselves; but our sufficiency is of God" 2 Corinthians 3:4-5.

We pray and hope that as husbands better know, and experience the sacrificial love of Christ, they will obey God and grow in the ability to express love to their wives in the name of Jesus. Amen.

QUESTION 63
WHAT ARE THE DUTIES OF A WIFE?

According to the Bible, the principal duty of a wife is to submit to her husband that is to be under the authority of her head – her husband - "Wives submit yourselves unto your own husbands, as unto the Lord. For the husband is the head of the wife, even as Christ is the head of the church and he is the savior of the body. Therefore as the church is subject to Christ, so let the wives be to their own husbands in everything: Ephes. 5: 22 - 24

The role of husband as the head, and a wife collaborating in submission to the husband were divinely established by God. This is clear from creation of man and woman, God first created the man, and then made the woman from the ribs of the man to be a suitable helper for him - Genesis 2:18. Apostle Paul explains the subjective roles of the wife and illustrates it well by using Christ and the church. As the church is subject to Christ, a wife is to be subject to the authority of her own husband. In her submissive disposition she acknowledges, recognizes, accepts and compliments the headship of the husband - "For the man is not of the woman: but the woman of the man. Neither was the man created for the woman; but the woman for the man" I Corinthians 11: 8-9.

A wife's submission to her husband's leadership is to be total – "in everything" which includes how she manages the household, the children, her career or business, her physical appearance, socio- cultural and spiritual dispositions. As Eve was created to complete Adam, a wife is to complement her husband physically, emotionally, socially, spiritually, intellectually and when the need arises financially. It is said that the wife is the manager of the home, but the husband is the manager of the wife. Just as the husband should be Christ like in his leadership, the wife has the privilege of being Christ like also in her role as a helper as she willingly serves her husband

The husband as a head needs all the help that he can get from the wife to fulfil the plan and purposes of God in the family in the areas of husbandry, fatherhood, career or business, social status and in ministry. As a "Helpmeet" whatever the woman does, her motive must be to help, compliment, complete, support, promote, encourage, motivate, uplift and project her husband. A very good example is given in the virtuous woman of the Bible according to the book of Proverbs chapter 31. A godly wife will do her best to work for the success of her husband as opposed to an insubordinate wife, who might be tempted to usurp, reject, question, grumble against, nag or undermine her husband's headship.

Finally in Titus 2:4-5 wives expected – "…to be sober, to love their husbands, to love their children, to be discreet, chaste, keepers at home, good, obedient to their own husbands, that the word of God be not blasphemed". A good wife will love her husband, be available for him sexually, be obedient to him, provide good, nutritious food for her husband, love and take good care of her children, keep the home, communicate with her husband often and be a good friend of her husband.

QUESTION 64
WHAT IS THE DIFFRENCE BETWEEN THE ROLE AND DUTY OF A WIFE?

A role is described as a set of expected or connected behaviors and obligations conceptualized by people in a social situation. Role is the functions assumed or the part played by a person in a particular situation. Synonyms or words having the same meaning with role are – position, job, task, duty, responsibility, part or function.

A duty is a moral or legal obligation, a responsibility; it is an act or a course of action that is required of one by position, social custom or religion. In other words – a responsibility, an obligation performed in obedience, a mark of commitment, loyalty, faithfulness and fidelity. In my role or position as a wife, I am duty bound to love and respect my husband. As a wife I am obliged to submit to my husband, support and compliment him in obedience to God, and a sign of my commitment, loyalty and faithfulness to my marriage vows. Practically the words – role, duty, and responsibility are the same in meaning but have slight differences when in use. They refer to the position,   expectation, and performance of a wife or husband in the family or society at large.

The role of a wife is who she is to her husband and her duty is what she does practically as the wife of her husband. The role of a wife is to submit to and compliment her husband in everything at home, at work and in the ministry because she is the wife. Her duties and responsibilities includes:-

Loving him and their children unconditionally

Being available for him physically and emotionally

Praying for him and with him, serving the Lord in togetherness

A good home keeper – cooking delicious meal for her husband and making every part of the home clean, neat and attractive

Hospitality – receiving and entertaining guess at home cheerfully, making people feel at home

Being a friend, confidant, ardent supporter and ever ready encourager in time of struggles

She not being idle or busybody; not a contentious woman, a nag or brawling woman at home – Prov. 25:24; 27:15.

But a virtuous woman   - Who respects and honor her husband. Her husband has confidence in her and her children are proud of her.

QUESTION 65
WHY IS IT DIFFICULT FOR SOME WOMEN TO SUBMIT TO

THEIR OWN HUSBANDS?

The Biblical injunction for wives to submit to their husband is clear –"Wives submit yourselves unto your own husbands, as unto the Lord. For the husband is the head of the wife, even as Christ is the head of the church and he is the savior of the body. Therefore as the church is subject to Christ, so let the wives be to their own husbands in everything: Ephes. 5: 22 - 24

This is not the idea of a male chauvinist - a product of a gender - biased, backward and patriarchal culture. Submission is part of God's design for marriage and it is applicable at all times and cultures because the word of God is infallible, it cannot be changed and it stands forever.

Many women are offended at the concept of submission because they misunderstand what the Bible actually teaches about the role – the position of a wife in the family. Every woman of God should understand why she was created and for what purposes. It is clear, the woman was created for the man. So without the man, there would have been no need of the woman. But God created the woman because she is needed, indispensable to the man. Without the woman, the first creature – the man cannot fulfill the plan and purposes of God for his life. That's why God said "It is not good for man to be alone", I will make him a helper, who will keep him company, fellowship with him and make him complete as a man – Genesis 2:18

The Bible goes on to say that since man cannot do it alone and he needs the help of the woman to serve him; and the woman cannot also do anything alone without the man, she should therefore recognize her role as a helper and serve her husband for God's sake. A woman is called to submit – to serve, to help the husband – whether the husband is good or bad, educated or illiterate, rich or poor. If a woman accepts the offer of marriage of a man, she is saying l am ready to do what God says l should do for you, not only because l love you, but most importantly because l love God and l want to fulfill the purpose for which God created me – I Corinthians 11: 11-12. All things are of God and everything should be done for God's sake.

Wherever there is an understanding, naturally, there will always be a performance.

Submission should be taught exactly as what it is, it is an attitude of love and service of a wife to the husband. Because the woman is to help and serve the husband, her ideas, opinions and contributions are highly needed and should be valued by the husband. The wife has a say in everything that concerns her family. As a helper to her husband, the husband should seek her opinion, listen to her, consider what she says and make her feel she is important, needed and she is playing her God-given role.

Biblical submission means that after a couple has discussed an issue, the husband has the responsibility under God to make the final decision. A godly wife will try to work for the success of whatever decision her husband makes. She will be glad and rejoice with the husband because she see herself as a partner in progress. She will be loyal to her husband, respect, honour him, encourage and support him in everything.

However, many women are married to men who are self-centered, egoistic, masochistic and even cruel to their wives. Everything in the house starts with such men, revolves round them and ends with them. Such men are still alone after marriage, while their wives are told what to do, where to go and what to say in everything. Their own idea of headship is for their wives to be commanded and ordered about doing what the husband want, when they want it and how they want it. This is far from biblical headship in the family as ordained by God.

The test of submission comes when a wife does not agree with her husband negative dispositions towards her. The struggle is intensified when the wife believes he is acting selfishly, and his decision may affect her and their children badly.

A wife in a difficult marriage must learn to depend on the Lord for her joy and satisfaction, rather than expecting to find ultimate fulfilment in her husband. She should pray for intervention and seek counsel. Offensive leaders believe they are always right, and everything should be done for their sake. As for them, it is their wives that need to be structured and be made conformable to their own type of headship. Some difficult husbands will even tell their wives that they as men don't need any counselor or any advice from anyone for that matter. Such wives should trust God, fast and pray for help from above, do all they can for God's sake, God will divinely intervene and all will be well.

QUESTION 66

THE HUSBAND AS THE HEAD IS SUPPOSED TO PROVIDE FOR THE FAMILY AND MY ROLE AS A WIFE IS TO SUPPORT HIM, BUT THE SITUATION IN MY HOME IS NOT LIKE THAT. AS A WIFE I AM PRACTICALLY THE ONE PROVIDING FOR MY FAMILY AND IT IS TELLING ON MY PHYSICALLY HEALTH AND MENTAL STABILITY,

WHAT AM I SUPPOSED TO DO?

To be the head of the family is not a joke at all, it is a place of responsibility, a place of sacrificial care and a place of certain tasks that must be done. It is the duty of a father as the head to meet the basic needs of the family – Food, Clothing, Shelter, Education, Nurture and care. The bible says in I Timothy 5:8 – "But if any provide not for his own, and especially for those of his own house, he hath denied the faith, and is worse than an infidel."

The bad economic situation in many society is affecting the headship of many husbands negatively. Some husbands got married while they were working and earning very good income, but unfortunately were laid off because their employers could not pay salaries anymore. Many companies are folding up, some are moving their businesses to other countries that are more viable; many small and medium scale enterprises have been wiped out and a lot of people are now jobless. But that is not an excuse for the head of the family to sit down and fold his arms, there must be a way out of joblessness and poverty.

It is written - "There hath no temptation taken you but such as is common to man: but God is faithful, who will not suffer you to be tempted above that ye are able; but will with the temptation also make a way to escape, that ye may be able to bear it". I Corinthians 10:13.

Husband's Lack of job or money must not be a permanent situation in the home. There are potential problems associated with husband's irresponsibility or lack of money, such as tension, quarrels, fear, poverty, sickness, misunderstanding and suspicion. These should not necessarily happen at home. The husband and wife should:-

Sit down, discuss and look for a way out

Fast and pray for God to make a way – a way of escape from poverty and lack, ask God to open your eyes to new way of making money, and give you ideas that will sell

If need be, the husband should retrain himself and get a new skill

Instead of waiting to be employed, be an employer by learning to produce something that we meet the need of people

Mind the way money is being spent – provide for your needs not wants

Don't spend more than you earn, do a budget, always safe some percentage of what you earn

Always pay your tithe, give offering and reach out to others in the church.

God will turn again your financial captivity, and it will be like a dream.

CELEBRATION IN THE BEDROOM – IMPORTANCE OF SEXUAL RELATIONSHIPBETWEEN HUSBAND AND WIFE

QUESTION 67

MY WIFE DOES NOT WANT SEX AT ALL, WHAT IS WRONG WITH HER?

Sex is good, biblical, Christianly, and it is spiritual. Sex is the gift of God for the married only. God created sex to be a blessing that should be mutually enjoyed by both husband and wife. Sex is a powerful means of communication between a husband and wife. It is a love language to express the fondness, oneness and the uniqueness of the marital relationship. Sex is God's appointed way for a husband and wife to reciprocally say to one another –'You are mine" "I belong to you completely, permanently and exclusively". Actually it is when a husband's rod (penis) enters into the wife's hole (Vagina); glued together in sexual ecstasy, that they are one physically inseparable entity in real sense. That is why a husband and why can be naked on their marital bed and not be ashamed.

Therefore shall a man leave his father and his mother, and shall cleave unto his wife and they shall be one flesh. And they were both naked, the man and his wife and were not ashamed. Genesis 2: 24 -25.

Why then should anyone – man or woman, be not interested in having sex? Is there not a cause? A wife in particular may avoid sex because of fear, former sexual abuse and negative religious bias against sex – seeing sex as carnal an evil. Some other reasons may include:-

Anxiety and fear due to painful sexual intercourse

Tiredness, stress and fatigue – due to the birth of a child and house keeping

Physical weakness due to headache, backache

Emotional disturbance – interpersonal relationship issue, conflict with husband or problem with children

Negative communication is a common cause of chronic conflict. Examples of negative communication include nagging, harsh criticism or 'stand over' tactics such as yelling to force compliance.

Poor communication, lack of intimacy and emotional satisfaction with husband

Erectile dysfunction and premature ejaculation on husband's side

Monthly period palaver – some women use their periods as an excuse to avoid sex, they are always on.

Poor personal hygiene – smelly partner – mouth and body odor, women get turned off by foul smells easily and bushy unclean shaved chin and chest

Lack of privacy – living in one room with children and others

Unsatisfying sex – lack of orgasm, un- pleasurable sex

Erroneous belief that sex is for having children only and not for pleasure

Sex hormone deficiency - due to menopause or old age

Good sex is right and not a privileged. It glues husband and wife together, it enhances intimacy and dependency. Husband and wife should work together and give themselves frequent, pleasurable and mutually enjoyable sex.

"Defraud ye not one the other except it be with consent for a time, that ye may give yourselves to fasting and prayer;

and come together again, that Satan tempt you not for your incontinency," I Corinthians 7:5.

QUESTION 68

MY HUSBAND HARDLY SPEAKS TO ME AFTER OUR MARRIAGE, BUT HE WAS NOT LIKE THAT BEFORE OUR WEDDING.

HOW CAN WE IMPROVE OUR COMMUNICATION?

Communication is the process of passing information verbally or non-verbally from one person to the other. Effective communication between husband and wife, parents and children is very important because it enables family members to express their feelings, ideas, needs, likes and dislikes, and concerns to each other. Communication is not just talking, it involves the ability to pay attention to what others are thinking and feeling, listening to what they have to say, understanding and responding to what they say accordingly.

It is very strange or odd for husband and wife to be together and not speak to each other. Poor communication is a common complaint of families who are having relational difficulties. Open and honest communication creates an atmosphere that allows husband and wife to express their differences as well as love and admiration for one another. It is through communication that family members are able to resolve the unavoidable problems that arise in all families. However, lack of communication or poor communication can lead to numerous family problems, including excessive family conflict, ineffective problem solving, lack of intimacy, physical and emotional separation. Good communication does not just happen, you have to work on it and make it happen.

There are many things that a husband and wife can do to become more effective communicators and in turn to improve the quality of their relationship. Here are some suggestions to follow:-

Continue in love - As the love of God has brought you together, continue to love each other unconditionally

Be friends of each other - as friends you will find it easy to speak, talk and discuss with each other freely

Communicate frequently – spend time with one another in meaningful conversation daily at home. When away from home, call each other on phone at least twice in a day, send texts messages just to say hello and keep in touch

Be positive, - Negative communication is the cause of unending conflict. Examples of negative communication include nagging, harsh criticism, name calling and tactics such as raising the voice and yelling to force compliance.

Communicate clearly and directly - Say what you mean and mean what you say. Indirect and vague communication will not only fail to resolve problems but will also contribute to lack of intimacy and emotional bonding

 Be an active listener - Active listening involves acknowledging and respecting the other person's point of view. Do your best to understand the point of view of the other person, as questions to clarify doubts.

Pay attention to non- verbal messages – Postures, gestures, signs, sighs and use of body parts used to communicate different messages as well, take note of them

Speak each other's love language – affirm in words, give gifts, spend quality time with each other and do things willingly for each other for love's sake

Pray for each other and watch

Communication is a key to successful marital relationship. Open and frequent communication is a mark or a sign of a happy, friendly, strong and healthy family relationship. While lack of communication or breakdown in communication show a breakdown in relationship, lack of intimacy and a sign of a family that is in trouble. Take necessary steps to improve the level of communication with your husband.

QUESTION 69
WHAT ARE THE HEALTH BENEFITS OF SEX?

Sex has been described as a tonic that brings vivacity and pleasure to the married as a glue that make husband and wife stick together at all times. Some people say when sex is right all will be right. This is because there are so many benefits of a mutually enjoyable sex on marital beds. Sexual intercourse between a wife and husband –

Is a very good physical exercise – a husband says it's like playing a football match

Helps keep their immune system strong – keeps sickness away from them

Boost their libido – having sex will make them to bond easily and enjoy the act regularly

Lowers blood pressure and the risk of heart attack

Reduces stress, lessens lower back and headache pains

Improves sleep – some use is as sleeping tablet! Laugh out loud! A man sleeps off immediately after the show

It lightens the mood - a wife that has been frowning will be all smiles after sex

May make prostate cancer less likely

Improves women's bladder control

Husband and wife should take pleasure in having sexual intercourse frequently. It reduces tension and fighting at home. It makes husband and wife to look forward seeing each other. Couples that have regular sex quarrel and fight less than those who don't.

Let thy fountain be blessed and rejoice with the wife of your youth. Let her be as the loving hind and a pleasant roe; let her breasts satisfy thee at all times;

and be thou ravished always with her love" Proverbs 5:18 - 19.

QUESTION 70
IS HUSBAND AND WIFE EQUALS?

Equality is defined as the condition of being equal, or the same in quality, measure, esteem or value. When men and women are both viewed as being just as smart and capable as each other, this is an example of equality of the sexes. There are different types of equality such as educational, political, social, legal, career, economic, and spiritual equality. There is a popular but controversial saying towards this effect- "what a man can do, a woman can even do better". According to this line of thought, equality stands for three basic features:-

Absence of special privileges in society – what is good for the goose is good for the gander.

Presence of adequate opportunities for development of all – no racial, sexual, socio – cultural bias – we have women doctors, lawyers ruler and presidents.

Equal satisfaction of basic needs of all – every one – men and women, young and old, boys and girls, educated or illiterate have basic needs like having a roof over the head, food on the table and clothes to put on, of course the social disposition and educational levels will make a difference in the time of the shelter, quality of food and food each can have.

Sincerely speaking can we really point to any society, whether in the developed and developing world nowadays where we have equality? Can your own society be called an equal, just and egalitarian society? No! Not in these days of – "Life of black matters" and gender induced violence. May God help us.

When it comes to marriage, it is an undebatable fact than a husband is higher and superior to the wife in many ways and in no way equal to him. God the founder of marriage made the differences between a man and his wife from the beginning. Even from natural order of things that we can see and observe, it is clear that the man is greater than the woman. Consider the followings facts -

The first to be created out of the dust by God is the man

The woman was created later, not from the dust but out of the man

As the head of the family – he is above and on top of the woman in God's organogram or hierarchy of the family. Apart from the Trinity, Husband is the number one member of the family.

The man is designed to give and wife is cut out to receive- the giver is always greater than the receiver, hand of the giver is always on top

Except for very few instances, the husband is normally physically strong, taller and bolder than the wife

The man is a determinant in the life and destiny of his wife, and children, for instance it is what he deposits into his wife that will germinate to be a boy or a girl. There is an adage in Yoruba language – "Agba osi ilu baje, baale ile ku, ile d'ahoro" - that is when elders are wanting in any society there will be corruption; and when a husband dies the family becomes desolate. Many lives and destiny have been truncated due to the death of a husband and a father.

The most natural way of a husband relating sexually with his wife is the man being on top! Call it missionary way, but that is the truth

When you look at the head physically – where are the eyes to see? The nose to smell? The ears to hear, the mouth to eat? They are all on the head – on the husband and father – who is the number one, the president of the family, the chief executive officer of the family affairs.

Naturally women look unto men for help and support.

I hope with all these points, I have been able to convince you and not confuse you that HUSBAND AND WIFE ARE NOT EQUALS. HUSBAND IS ON TOP.

In God, in Christianity men and women are equals by the virtue of what Jesus did for us – paying the penalty of sin on the cross, giving us justification and eternal life by his resurrection – "For we are all children of God by faith in Christ Jesus. There is neither Jew nor Greek, there is neither bond or free, there is neither male nor female for ye are all one in Christ Jesus." Galatians 3: 26, 28.

Men and women were created by God and they both have the breadth of God in them. Salvation through Christ is for both man and woman who dares to believe in Jesus and accept Him as personal Lord and Saviour. God is pouring out His Holy Spirit upon men and women even in these latter days, and both men and women will go to the same heaven at last. In that wise we are all equals before God.

QUESTION 71

I AM A NURSING MOTHER WITH TWO CHIDREN MY HUSBAND WANTS

SEX ALLMOST EVERYDAY, IS IT NORMAL?

This question sounds familiar with people of your age and experience in marriage. After having a baby or two the stress of having to cater for children and housekeeping make some women to be less interested in sex at this period of childbearing and child raising.

There is nothing really wrong with your husband's desire to relate with you sexually every day.

The only time it is not okay is if you do not want to have sex for a genuine reason, or if having sex gets in the way of your day to day activities. For example if your family devotion and prayer life is being hindered by this act, or sex is making your husband to lose focus spiritually and career wise, then you have to sit down and discuss how to curtail his sexual desires and regulate the frequency of your sexual intercourse.

Many people go through stages in their lives where they want to have more sex, less sex and even no sex at all – time changes things. It is actually not common for couple to have sex every day, may be once in a day and few times in a week. As long as both of you are comfortable physically and emotionally, have as much sex as you want. But there are certain uncomfortable physical situations that can arise from having too much sex. Most of the time when these happen women don't want to have sex anymore if possible.

A woman can experience vaginal tears due to dryness as a result of too much sex. This will make sexual intercourse painful. A lot of sex can cause a urinary tract or vaginal infection if care is not taken. There can be irritation or rashes on the external skin around the vulva, and the labia could become engorged and swollen. The husband can also experience pain, irritation, and soreness from too much sex. Ejaculating every day will also cause pain and discomfort to the husband. Apart from the unpleasant physical symptoms, there are also psychological aspect of having too much sex. A wife may be overwhelmed by the expectation to perform sexually more than the husband, and this pressure can cause withdrawal and resentment.

Husband if you wife is saying you are having too much sex, then you might be that your sex drive is too high. It is also possible that you are using sex as a form of escapism or as a coping mechanism. If you have no job currently, or you have a psychological disturbance, sex may be used to cover a deeper problem. If you are on drug you may have to stop it. You need to examine yourself and know why you have excessive sexual drive. Excess of anything is bad, you need to be concerned about how your wife feels. Sex should be fun and be mutually enjoyable, not a causer of anxiety or bodily injury.

"Let the husband render unto the wife due benevolence;

and likewise also the wife unto the husband. …Defraud ye not one another, except it be with consent for a time, that ye may give yourselves to fasting and prayer, and come together again, that Satan tempt you not for your incontinency" I Corinthians 7: 3, 4.

QUESTION 72

WHY ARE SOME WIVES SO REBELLIOUS, EVEN AMONG

CHRISTIANS WOMEN?

Hun! Big question! Does it not sound contradictory to have rebellious Christian wives?

Since the fall of man in the Garden of Eden, Men and women have been disobedient to God, blame shifting, faultfinding, rebellious against husbands, bitterness against wives and pointing accusing fingers at each other. Thank God for the grace of our Lord Jesus Christ that saved us from the power of sin. Obviously, we cannot be in sin and say grace should abound. Never! Every rebellious wife should repent, confess and forsake the sin of rebellion. "For rebellion is as the sin of witchcraft, and stubbornness is as iniquity and idolatry." I Samuel 15: 23a.

What is rebellion? It is the action or process of resisting constituted authority, control or convention. It is an act of disobedience to established rules and regulations in a secular, governmental, spiritual, social and cultural situation. In the marriage or family context it is opposition to the husband as a head and leader of the family. It is the refusal of the wife to submit to the leadership of the husband and obey his instructions. This is grievous and unacceptable before the Lord God Almighty who ordained marriage.

A rebellious wife likes to usurp and challenge the authority of the husband. She goes against the biblical rules that govern the family relationship. A wife who fights and shouts at the husband at all times is rebellious. A wife who abuses her husband at the least provocation, who argues blindly, complains bitterly and allows corrupt communications to proceed out of her mouth against her husband when in conflict is a rebel of the highest order. It is written - "Let no corrupt communication proceed out of your mouth, but that which is good to the use of edifying, that it may minister grace to the hearers" Ephesians 4:29. "And I say unto you, that every idle word that men shall speak, they shall give account thereof in the Day of Judgment" Mathew 12:36.

Such a woman stands the risks or danger of disaster. Diseases and sicknesses such as high blood pressure, heart attack, mental and emotional breakdown due to constant stress of vital organs of the body are not far from her. A rebellious woman is contentious and nervous and knows no peace nor joy in the Holy Spirit. She becomes an embarrassment to the husband, a disappointment to neighbors, a bad example for the children, a disgrace to womanhood and Christendom. If special care is not taken, the marriage may end in a long separation, and finally in divorce. God forbid bad thing. Of a truth, - "It is better to dwell in the corner of the housetop, than with a quarrelsome wife in a big house. Proverbs 25:24.

What will make a professing Christian wife become rebellious against God and the authority of her husband? Something is wrong somewhere. It may be that the woman out of anger, bitterness, and unforgiveness against her husband has become so overwhelmed with these negative emotions to the extent that she could no longer control herself. "He that hath no rule over his own spirit is like a city that is broken down and without walls"

Under this situation such a wife has opened doors to all sorts of satanic and demonic influences and attacks. The husband in love should not put up any "I don't care attitude" "I am the head here" or "a holier than thou attitude". He should intercede for his wife, take authority over foul spirits, plead the blood of Jesus over the body soul and spirit of his wife and ask God for mercy on both of them. He should prayerfully counsel the wife to avoid such attitude.

It takes two to tango. The husband may have contributed to this situation by neglecting his wife, not loving her enough, not dealing with her as a delicate or weaker vessel and wanting to exercise authority over her by force by fire. The husband should ask his wife why she is behaving uncomely towards him, and listen to her without trying to justify himself or looking for an escape root for himself. The husband should ask God to open his inner eyes to see what exactly is going on in his relationship with the wife. He should love his wife unconditionally, recognize her role as a wife and allow her room enough to be able to perform her duties as a helper suitable to him. "Husband, love your wives, and be not bitter against them" Colossians 3: 19.

Husband and wife should obey God and follow His commandments concerning marriage. Whenever there is problem, it is the Devil at work – he comes to steal, kill and destroy. Husband and wife should submit to God, resist the Devil by taking care of each other, being watchful and prayerful. If the husband and wife can work as a theme, the Devil will run and leave the family alone. There shall be confession of sin and repentance, there shall be forgiveness and acceptance and the peace of God will return to the family. The beauty of marital love will manifest in wife's submission to and reverence of the husband, instead of rebellion in the name of Jesus. Amen.

QUESTION 73
MY HUSBAND IS VERY HARSH AND RATHER TOO RASH!

HOW DO I DEAL WITH THIS SITUATION?

A harsh person is someone who is severe or strict. Such people have the tendency be unpleasant in action or effect.

They act too hastily or without due consideration. From all indications l guess your husband is a difficult person. You have to learn how to deal with difficult people because sometimes they are impossible to avoid. By 'difficult' people we mean people with certain personality traits or emotional characteristics that make it difficult for others to communicate or relate well with them.

Sometimes people can be difficult because they seem to have a need to exaggerate the things that happen to them or bring drama into almost any situation that they can. If this is the root of a difficult person's problems then you may need help dealing with attention-seeking adults. There are many different types of difficult people. We need to identify some of the different types so that you can know the best way to interact with them.   Think about your husband and figure out which category (ries) he belongs to among these groups-

"Downers also known as negatives" – They always have something bad to say. They complain, murmur, criticize, and judge others. They are offensive and almost impossible to please. They are angry, very anxious, pessimistic and very critical of others

"Better Thans also known as know it Alls" – They are fond of comparing themselves with others. They are envious jealous people. They talk so much about themselves and enjoy showing off and like to impress people a lot.

"Egoists" - They are very selfish, their own interests come first. They are hyper- sensitive to personal affronts, they are rejection – sensitive, easily offended and may be ungrateful even when you have strived to help them.

"Passives" – also known as Push- overs, Yes men and weaklings. They   are somehow indolent, they don't contribute much to conversations and let others do the hard work,

"Tanks also are known as being explosive"   They are handful, or bossy. They want their way and will do anything to get it.

"Hostiles" – Hostile people tend to react always violently. They can be cynical, scornful, and argumentative. They are always right, and have trouble being in the wrong. They like power tussles and very rank or status conscious.

How do you deal with them? The way to relate well with a difficult person is to try understand where they are coming from. It is inevitable for you to come across a difficult person in your life that bring about distress, whether it's in the form of a neighbor, relative, colleague, employee, customer, or supplier. However, the intensity of their difficulty may vary depending upon the kind of difficult person they are; downers, better thans, passives, or tanks. Try to find their value language. A value language is what someone values most. It is what drives their decisions. For some people it is money; for others, it is position, power or knowledge and the crave to be recognized or be in charge.

Don't try to change them. No one can rely change any other person, only God can do that through his word and by the power of the Holy Spirit – "For the word of God is quick, and powerful and sharper than any two edged sword, piercing even to the diving asunder of soul and spirit, and of the joints and marrow, and is a discerner of the thoughts and intents of the heart" Hebrews 4:12.

The Bible says the heart of man is desperately wicked, no one can know it but the word of God exposes our innermost thoughts and desires. Difficult people need a change of heart, they need to put off the old self and put on the newness of life in Christ. They need to put off anger, bitterness, complaining, judging others and avenging themselves. They should let God have his ways in their lives and in their marital relationships. God is able to bring about a change of a stony heart to a heart of flesh. –"The king's heart is in the hand of the Lord, as the rivers of water, he turneth it whithersoever he will" Proverbs 21:1.

Living with difficult people could be discouraging and enervating. We need to pray for divine intervention because prayer changes thing- "Be anxious for nothing, but in everything by prayer and supplication, with thanksgiving, let your requests be made known to God; and the peace of God, which surpasses all understanding, will guard your hearts and minds through Christ Jesus" Philippians 4: 6-7. Sometimes when we try to encourage Downers to be more positive, Passives to stand up for themselves, Tanks to calm down, and Better Thans to be more humble - they become defensive, resentful and get worse.

Avoid raising your voice all the time with them – don't engage in shouting, screaming, and brawling, it will only increase tension and show that you've lost control. Always stay calm, and if you feel yourself getting angry, just walk away

Don't let them be toxic – toxic people are master manipulators, skilled liars and great actors. Toxic relationships are harmful, any time you have to deal with them you feel exhausted, emotionally drained and stressed. Anyone who is abusive, unsupportive and who basically say or do things that discourage more than bringing you up is toxic. Whenever we are faced with unreasonably difficult people, our instinct is to react with frustration and irritation. That, however, is the ticket to emotional instability. It causes tension to build at home, can prove a serious threat to marital relationship as well as the overall stability of the family.

Toxicity can manifest in many behavior, toxic people:-

Create and are surrounded by interpersonal problems

Try to manipulate and control people

Are needy and make strong demands on other people's attention

Are critical of themselves and extremely critical of other people

Do not want to seek help or try to change

Could be disrespectful and always seem to get their way.

Stay positive and go for counseling – "Where there is no counsel, the people fall, but in the multitude of counsellors there is safety. Proverbs 15:22.

Finally, people say it takes two to tango. Dear wife, you may have to examine your own actions and reactions at home too. It may be that you husband is reacting to some attitudes of yours. You may also need to pray the prayer of David –"Search me, o God and know my heart, try me, and know my thoughts; and see if there be any wicked way in me, and lead me in the way everlasting." I believe this and other things will be sorted our during counseling, by the grace of God.

Thanks! Thanks!

QUESTION 74

MY WIFE AND I DO LOVE EACH OTHER BUT RECENTLY SHE SEEMS TO BE DISTANCING HERSELF FROM ME AND WOULD NOT WANT TO DO ANYTHING TOGETHER WITH ME, WHAT COULD BE THE REASONS FOR THIS CHANGE?

In a lighter mood, in these days of Covid 19 – Corona virus pandemic, social distancing is encouraged even at home to prevent virus infection. This may be one of the reasons why your wife is distancing herself from you. On a serious note, there is no causeless course, there must be a reason or reasons why she is distancing herself physically and emotionally as well. We will need to figure it out.

God created marriage to solve the problem of loneliness, it is not good for a husband or wife to be alone. Marriage is for fellowship, for companionship and for cordial relationship in togetherness. Husband and wives are supposed to be the closest to each other, an inseparable entity- "… And they two shall be one flesh: so then they are no more two two, but one flesh. What therefore God has joined together, let not man put asunder" Mark 10:8-9.

Having become one flesh, it is expected that husband and wife will do many things together such as –

Pray together – they should pray together early in the morning and at the end of each day thanking God together. If possible husband and wife should join hands together when praying. It is a sign of oneness and agreement. It is written – "And I tell you more whenever two of you on earth agree about anything you pray for, it will be done for you by my Father in heaven. Mathew 18:19. "One shall chase a thousand two shall put ten thousand to fight" Deuteronomy 32:30.

Sleep together - in the same room on the same bed – it enhances intimacy and bonding. "If it is cold, two can sleep together and stay warm, but how you can keep warm by yourself" Ecclesiastes 4:11. When a husband and wife sleep together, they have the opportunity to look at each other and see into each other. They can talk, discuss, share information, resolve quarrel and pending matters can easily be attended to amicably. "Two people can resist an attack that would defeat one person alone, A rope made of three cords – (husband, wife and the Trinity) is hard to break" Eccles. 4:12.

Have sex regularly – Couples who are friendly and close to each other will frequently and mutually enjoy sex. Sex is the lubricant that oils the wheel of marriage and keeps it running smoothly. Sex is a non-verbal language of love and a very good indication of closeness or togetherness. When husband and wife relate often sexually they are saying to each other - "l love you: "I need you", "I want you" "I am satisfied without you", "I am prepared to spend the rest of my life with you" and that "There can be no one else but you" "It's only you" in this act of love.

Eat together – It is a sign of affection and closeness to each other. If possible eat together on the same plate, it gives husband and wife a sense of belonging. It makes them look forward to seeing each other. A couple should eat together at least once in a day, on the same table at the same time.

Bathe together – This is fun and romantic. Husband and wife should cultivate the habit of bathing together. This should be done as often as possible, most especially at night when the children are already in bed. By the time husband and wife are left alone, experiencing empty nest – when all children are gone to their own respective marital homes, bathing together should be a common practice.

Going out together – Husband and wife should always go out together unless it has to do with official, business or career matter. They should attend church services together, social gatherings, family meetings, invitation to functions and any other important occasion together. This will block the idea of someone else being physically and emotionally too close to your spouse in your absence - siting, talking, gisting, laughing, joining hands in prayer, with your spouse. Many aspiring singles are cautioned when they see a man with his wife beside him or a woman with her husband right by her side.

Dress in the same attire – This is a socio – cultural habit that it is gradually being wiped out nowadays. The Yoruba people of south west Nigeria have this culture of husband and wife dressing in the same traditional attire, cut out mostly in "Iro and Buba" - for the wife and in "Buba, sokoto and Agbada" for the husband. In this way, husband and wife are easily identified, they look special and it makes them unique in appearance. I know one of our big daddies and mummies in the Lord that are always dressed in the same attire at all social or cultural occasions. Even when they go to church and dressed in English way, their clothes match in colour. This is beautiful! It is a sign of oneness, they are happy to be seen and recognized as one.

Minister together - inside and outside of their own church. There is danger in "Powerful Ministers" going out to minister alone without their spouses. The enemy has messed up the ministry and even driven out many husbands and wives out of the ministry for doing it alone – physically and emotionally. Your closest person in the ministry should be your spouse.

Having said all, why would a spouse not want to be together in these areas and others?

In reality couple who are in conflict or have many unresolved problems, have the tendency to keep away from each other, because they are angry and not happy with each other. That is why the Bible says _"Be angry but do not sin, do not let the sun go down on your anger, and do not make room for the devil" Ephesians 4:26-27.

Dear husband, your wife may be angry with you for one reason or the other. Call your wife tell her what you have noticed in your relationship, ask her if there are any ways you have offended her. Quickly resolve your problems, apologize where necessary, forgive and forget the past and move on to a glorious future in togetherness.

"Let all bitterness, and wrath, and anger and clamor, and evil speaking, be put away from you, with all malice. And be ye kind one to another, tenderhearted, forgiving one another, even as God for Christ's sake hath forgiven you".

Ephesians 4: 31-32.

QUESTION 75
HOW OFTEN SHOULD A MARRIED COUPLE HAVE SEX?

God created sex to be a blessing for both husband and wife to enjoy within marriage. God designed the sexual union as the sign of a husband and wife's unique commitment to each other. In general, the Bible teaches that married couples should have sex regularly. Sex is perhaps the most powerful God –created way to help a couple give entire self to the other. Sex is a powerful language of love. It is a way for husband and wife to reciprocally say to one another- "I love you, I belong to you, I am completely, permanently and exclusively yours". When couples stop having sex, their relationships become vulnerable to anger, detachment, infidelity and, ultimately, divorce.

"Now concerning the things whereof ye wrote unto me: It is good for a man not to touch a woman. Nevertheless, to avoid fornication, let every man have his own wife, and let every woman have her own husband. Let the husband render unto the wife due benevolence: and likewise also the wife unto the husband. The wife hath not power of her own body, but the husband: and likewise also the husband hath not power of his own body, but the wife. Defraud ye not one the other, except it be with consent for a time, that ye may give yourselves to fasting and prayer; and come together again, that Satan tempt you not for your incontinency" I Corinthians 7: 1-5

There may be no one right answer to the question of how often couples should have sex. The answers can range from once a week to twice a month. It is advisable for couples to try and do it at least once in a week. A couple's sex life is affected by so many different factors such as - age, lifestyle, each spouse's health and natural libido and, of course, the quality of their overall marital relationship. Sex is important to married couples. It is the glue that keeps them together and without it, couple become "good friends" at best, or "bickering roommates" at worst. Most sexual problems are relationship problems. The key to building sexual intimacy is to build personal intimacy in your marriage relationship. The quality of your relational intimacy will shape your sexual intimacy. When we don't connect well on the inside we are not likely to connect well on the outside.

Husband and wife should be friends, a friend loves at all times. Some husbands overlook or neglect cultivating such a friendship with their wives. Consequently they don't relate well sexually, because she is tempted to feel that the husband is merely using her body, while not really caring for her personally. Some couples almost never come together sexually because of unresolved conflicts that have led to bitterness and relational distance. Angry husbands withhold sexual affection as a way of punishing their wives too. That is not good at all. Godly love finds great pleasure in giving pleasure to the beloved. The husband must fulfill his duty to his wife, and likewise also the wife to her husband.

QUESTION 76
CAN A WIFE INNITIATE SEX?

A wife can initiate sex- that is, make the husband feel like relating sexually with her when she likes it. There is nothing wrong in a wife showing in action or asking her husband to relate with her sexually when she is the mood. She is giving her body to her husband which is part of her duty as a wife. Initiating sex should not always fall on one spouse only, because being wanted makes a husband or wife feel important and all right. One of a man's deepest emotional needs is to feel that his wife desires him. And if he sees that his wife desires him, it gives him a sense of well-being in all other areas of his life. However, while it is appropriate for a wife to initiate sexual relations, God's general design in marriage is for a husband to lead and a wife to respond.

Initiating sex is an important part of marital relationship where sex means a lot to both of them. Sex was created by God as something beautiful, meaningful and pleasurable to be mutually enjoyed by the husband and wife. Some couples have a mild way of telling their spouses they want sex. Statements such as "I want to come to my garden"/ "Would you mind coming to your garden?" "I would like to go to Jerusalem" "Will you come with me to Jerusalem?" "I would like to feel you" " "I 'm at home for you" "Come away my love" are subtle of initiating sex, or telling your spouse verbally that you are in the mood. A very good example of a woman seeking for her husband and would not let him go until she brought him to bed is found in the love story of the Shulamite girl and her shepherd lover. - Song of Solomon 3: 1-5 - "By night on my bed, I sought him…but 1 found him whom my soul loveth; I held him, and would not let him go, until I had brought him into the chamber"

People say actions speak louder than voices. A woman can initiate sex by doing any or some of the following:-

Being extra ordinarily nice to the husband during the day. Cooking his favorite dishes, an intimate phone call, smiling broadly when he returns home and doting around him are attractive sex signals that cannot be ignored.

Looking sexually attractive – wearing clothes and nightwear that your husband finds exciting – he will notice this and you may move unusually closer to him

Going to bed with a transparent nightgown without undies – pant and bra, your husband will invariably discover this and will not rest until it is over

When on bed cuddle up against him, begin to caress and fondle him, it will lead to sex

You can get naked when you are alone with him, intentionally drop something you have to bend down and pick before his full glare, you are likely to end up in bed without even picking up anything again

Ask if he would like to take a shower with you, give him a passionate hug and kisses, when out of the shower, and lie in bed completely naked with your thighs parted to show your pubic hair and your buttocks.

Offer to give your husband a massage, until you end up massaging his inner thighs.

When sex is mutually enjoyed by husband and wife, it does not really matter who or how sex is initiated. Husband and wife should learn and try to be more romantic in their marriage. It is true that sex is the oil that lubricates the wheel of marriage, and make it runs smoothly.

QUESTION 77

HELP! OURS IS A SEXLESS MARRIAGE! MY HUSBAND IS ALWAYS HAVING ONE SICKNESS OR THE OTHER TO AVOID SEX,

WHAT CAN I DO?

It is common for a couple to have different levels of sexual desire. However, when one partner shuts the door on sex in a marriage, it can have devastating effects on the other spouse emotionally and psychologically. Sexual experience is always a synergy of biological, psychological and social factors. There are many reasons why men can lose their sex drive, this is called sexual dysfunctions in men. Some of these problems can often be resolved by treating the underlying issues such as marital or relationship problems, feeling of guilt for unconfessed sin of adultery or fornication; Work related stress; depression, and anxiety, emotional distancing, lack of communication and unresolved conflict with a spouse.

Sexual dysfunction is any physical or psychological problem that prevents a spouse from giving or getting sexual satisfaction. This problem can affect men of all ages, but is common with increasing age. The most common problems related to sexual dysfunction in men are;-

Low libido – reduced sexual desire or no interest in sex. May be due to low testosterone level of the male sex hormone, it affects sex drive and sperm production. Hormone shots, pills or creams may help improve sexual function by increasing blood flow to the penis.

Erectile dysfunction – having difficulty in getting and keeping an erection for sexual intercourse. This could be frustrating, there cannot be physical sex relationship without erection.

Premature ejaculation – ejaculation that occurs before or too soon after penetration.

Inhibited or delayed ejaculation – ejaculation does not happen or takes a very long time.

Sex in marriage is not just about the libido of a spouse. It is the divine duty of a husband to have sexual intercourse regularly with his wife. God created sexual intercourse in marriage for procreation and for the pleasure and enjoyment of both husband and wife. There will be no children without sex, this unfortunately accounts for some of the childlessness we witness in some marriages. Some couples who have no children, often allow quarrels and misunderstandings to prevent them from relating sexually at the time when the wife is most fertile.

For women, sex is more than just an act. I Peter 3:7 encourages husbands to dwell with their wives according to knowledge. The implication of this is that spouses should perform their God-given duty sexually, this is something which only they can do for each other. Any health or medical issue can easily be resolved medically and spiritually when husbands and wives are kind, considerate and selfless.

Husbands should take note that ejaculating more often could lower your risk of prostate cancer and make you generally healthier according to researchers. Good eating habit, healthy life style, regular aerobic exercise and strength training can increase your stamina, improve body image and boost libido.

QUESTION 78
MY WIFE DOES NOT LIKE KISSING, WHY?

Kissing and hugging are practical physical ways of expressing affection, displaying the emotion of love. For lovers it's the first moment of physical intimacy. Passionate kissing between a husband and wife could initiate sexual intimacy. Frequent kiss will lead to less stress, more relationship satisfaction, and also a decrease in bad cholesterol level. Clearly, just like sex, socio-cultural background may affect the frequenting of kissing and hugging among couples. You can hardly find African couples displaying such emotion, most especially in public. Kissing is encouraged to promote intimacy and affection between couples. If a husband enjoys kissing, the wife should gradually work on herself, tune her mind to and flow with this form of communication as well.

If a wife does not like kissing, do not force it on her. It might be due to any of these following reasons:-

She may just not be comfortable with it because of her background. You can encourage her gradually, till she gets used to it.

It might be because of the husband's bad oral hygiene. Make sure your breath is fresh and inviting anytime you want to kiss her.

May not want to show physical affection – lack of physical affection like kissing or hugging is an indication of relationship problem. Emotional distancing, lack of closeness or intimacy may be due to unresolved conflict, bitterness or anger against you, try and manage conflicts and resolve marital disputes as they occur

She may be in bad mood due to pains – stress, headache, or backache, menstrual pain.

It could be a sign that she does not enjoy your kissing – hard or patched lips, too much saliva, unclean shave with beards that pinch and bad breath, may have put her off.

 In any case, husband and wife should bring romance to their marriage. Encourage intimacy by taking good care of personal hygiene and learn to kiss properly. Everywoman

Should be like the Shulamite woman of the Songs of Solomon 1:2 "Let him kiss me with the kisses of his mouth! For your love is more delightful than wine." Here are some health benefits of kissing:-

It opens up blood vessels

Lowers blood pressure

Increased heart rate burn calories

It boots your happy hormones and leave you feeling so good

It relieves stress, and reduces anxiety

It helps relieves cramps and soothes headaches

It boots your immune system and reduces allergic response

It boots sex drive

Love expressed openly and physically, changes people for good. The act of kissing can have a positive impact on your emotional and physical wellbeing. Kissing makes both parties feel good about themselves and can help strengthen relationships, so kiss and kiss often. It's good for you!

CHILD BREARING AND CHILD REARING

QUESTION 79
WHY CAN'T I HAVE MY OWN BABY?

When God created the man and made the woman from his rib, He also gave them the authority to be fruitful and multiply. This involves having children to continue the progeny of the human race. The psalmist in Psalm 127 says - "Lo, children are an heritage of the Lord; and the fruit of the womb is his reward…Happy is the man that hath his quiver full of them". There is no gainsaying in the fact that children gladden the heart of their parents and they are future defence. That is why couples who are yet to have children are anxious about the situation. There is no cause for alarm, it is written there shall be no barren in the land. The word of God is forever settled in heaven, His word must surely come to pass.

A couple who have sex regularly should be having their first child after one year of marriage. But some have delay in child birth for some reasons. Infertility is when a woman have trouble getting pregnant or staying pregnant. Fertility problems can happen in women and men. Causes of infertility in women includes:-

Lack of ovulation – not releasing eggs from ovaries, won't be able to get pregnant

Blocked fallopian tube – so sperm cannot swim to fertilize the eggs released from the ovaries

Poor egg quality – not being able to get fertilized

Shape of the uterus – makes it hard for a fertilized egg to be implanted

Miscarriage –

Untreated chlamydia or gonorrhea

Uterine fibroids

Endometriosis – a painful condition where the tissue lining the uterus, called the endometrium, grows in places other than inside the uterus. Age related – age impacts egg quality as well as quantity.

In women, sign of infertility may include – pain during sex, heavy, long or painful periods, chronic pelvic pain, back pains, dark or pale menstrual blood, irregular menstrual cycle, hormone changes, underlying medical conditions – damage to fallopian tubes or ovaries , obesity or being underweight, cancer and cancer treatments.

Infertility affects both men and women. Both husband and wife should be tested for infertility if a couple is having trouble getting pregnant.   Male infertility rarely has symptoms that are observable without a semen analysis. This will measure the health condition of the semen and sperm. Most common causes of infertility in men include:-

Untreated chlamydia or gonorrhea

Low sperm count – not having enough sperm in the semen

Poor sperm movement – sperm does not swim well enough to reach an egg

Problem with ejaculation – ejaculation can send semen into bladder, instead of out of the penis.

Injury to the scrotum and testes

Overheated testicles from wearing clothing that's too tight, swimming or bathing in hot water regularly.

Life style factors – excessive drug or alcohol use, smoking cigarettes

Lots of exposure to environmental toxins like lead or pesticides

Every couple looking forward to having their baby should learn to wait on the Lord. Couple should seek relevant medical checkup and care while waiting. I assure you that God who gave couples the authority to be fruitful and multiply is still on the throne. He is the same, yesterday today and forever. Relax, God is in full control. Be patience, be anxious for nothing, praise God and let your heart desires be made known to him in prayers. For with God nothing shall be impossible Luke 1:37.

QUESTION 80
CAN I ADOPT A CHILD? IS ADOPTION A CHRISTIAN ACT?

There are two ways to have children – the first way is through natural conception and delivery and the second way is through adoption. Adoption is the act of taking something on as your own. Adoption usually refers to the legal process of becoming a non- biological parent. It is the noun form of adopt, meaning to choose for oneself. It creates a parent-child relation between people that are not blood related. The adopted child is entitled to all privileges belonging to the biological child or children of the adoptive parents, including the right to inherit.

Adoption is a biblical, Old Testament and New Testament practice. God called father Abraham in Genesis Chapter 12:1-3; and promised to make a nation out of him. God Himself adopted Israel, He chose Jacob for Himself the descendant of Abraham as promised – Isaiah 41: 8-10; - "Who are Israelites, to whom pertaineth the adoption, and the glory and the covenants, and the giving of the law, and the service of God, and the promises" Romans 9:4

Moses was an adopted son of Pharaoh's daughter in Egypt. Pharaoh's daughter took Moses as her own son and he enjoyed royalty in Egypt until God's plan and purpose for his life was revealed. There was no question of his heritage of worthiness. He simply belonged, as it should be in any adoption. He grew up as an Egyptian until He had to leave Egypt to fulfil divine purpose for his life. "At that time Moses was born, and he was no ordinary child. For three months he was cared for by his family. When he was placed outside, Pharaoh's daughter took him and brought him up as her own son. Moses was educated in all the wisdom of the Egyptians and was powerful in speech and action." Acts 7:20 -22.

Adoption in Christian theology is the admission of a believer into the family of God – Ephesians 1:5-6 –"Having predestinated us unto the adoption of children by Jesus Christ to himself, according to the good pleasure of his will, to the praise of the glory of his grace, wherein he hath made us accepted in the beloved". All Christians are adopted children of God by grace through faith in Christ Jesus. Ga; 4:5, Rom 1:8, Rom 8:15, Rom 9:4. It is by adoption that all of us came to be part of God's family, and have the right to call God our Father – "For ye have not received the spirit of bondage again to fear; but ye have received the spirit of adoption whereby we cry Abba, Father"

There are many advantages of adoption some of them are:-

You become a parent – you will have somebody to call you daddy or mummy.

Adoption make you feel like a normal human being. The reproach of barrenness is removed.

Adoption removes the pain and stress caused by infertility, and all the medical challenges, expenses and struggles to get a child.

As a woman, adoption saves you the trouble of conception, pregnancy, labor and delivery with all the risks danger and pains associated.

Adoption brings joy, laughter and peace to the family, adopted children make their parents fulfilled.

You have someone to share your life and properties with, you have a heritage.

God will reward those who adopt children. Adoption is receiving a stranger who has no real home into your life and family. You are giving the child mother care, love and basic needs of life – " And the King will answer and say to them, Assuredly, I say to you, in as much as you did it to one of the least of these brethren, you did it to me" Mathew 25:40.

Adoption also has its challenges as well. In these days of deceit, child trafficking and kidnapping children for sale, finding a child to adopt is very difficult. That notwithstanding, if you are determined to have a child through adoption, pray to God, seek and you will find your own to adopt. You need to make up your mind not to listen or give ears to gossips and backbiters. Some mean people may tell you to your face that the child or children you have were not born by you. Make sure you adopt a child or children legally and have your paper intact. Be prepared for any false accusation from any quarters.

Most importantly, you need to tell your adopted child at an early age, as soon as he or she can understand that you are a special care taker of him or her, that you are not the biological parents. This early information in a loving way, will protect your child from growing up to receive the news from outside. The shock could be destructive. The situation should be made clear to the child. As husband and wife you hoped to have children of your own to love and care for, but they were not forth coming. As for the child the parents could not give proper care for him or her. So both of you are meeting each other's need in adoption. Even if the biological parents show up in future, the child already know the background situation. He is not likely to turn his or her back on you because of what you have been to and done for him or her.

Your adopted child may become disobedient or a problem child. That should not discourage you. If you have had your own biological children, they may even do worse things. We all have been disobedient to God but he never disowned us for that. Pray and show love to this child. God will touch the heart and he will be a source of joy and blessing to your family.

Couples who have been trying to have children for years and could not should adopt a child or children legally. Find out where you may be able to get a child to adopt, for instance an orphanage. It is very possible to adopt a baby in less than one year. Plan with an adoption lawyer who can educate you about the process of adoption in your society or nation. Know that everything in life involves risk. Believe that this child is God's blessing to your life.

Celebrate your adopted child. Train the child in every way. Have celebrations for birthday, graduation and others, just as you would have done for a biological child. "Delight thyself also in the Lord: and he shall give thee the desires of thine heart. Commit thy way unto the Lord and he shall give thee the desires of thine heart". Psalm 37: 4-5.

QUESTION 81
IS BIRTH CONTROL PERMITTED FOR CHRISTIANS?

Genesis 1; 27 -28 make it clear that God created marriage for procreation. Husband and wives have been given divine authority to be fruitful and multiply. Children are God's heritage, sources of happiness and a kind of defence in future –Psalm 127. Why then should we control childbearing? We have to control how many children we bring into this world and when they are to come for obvious reasons. Birth control is not a sin against God. It is simply a responsible parenthood. Nowadays, unlike before, it is no longer –"as many" as 1 am able to produce! But – "how well "can 1 nurture and take proper care of them? So that they don't become neglected, abandoned and cast away due to lack of parental care; roaming, combing the streets and becoming a nuisance to the society.

Birth control is good and spiritual. It is sitting down to count the cost and planning to have successful childbearing, childrearing and parenting in the family. It is the practice of preventing unwanted pregnancies, especially by the use of contraception. It is the use of any practices, methods, or devices to prevent pregnancy from occurring. Birth control is Planned Parenthood. It is not just having children as many as you can, but it is having the number of Children you want to have and when you want them. It is not a sin it is rather a sign of spiritual maturity, social responsibility and understanding.

Beyond preventing unwanted pregnancy, birth control has lots of benefits for women

It regulates menstrual cycles

It makes periods less painful

Helps to regulate hormonal acne

It reduces the risk of uterine cancer

It reduces the risk of ovarian cyst

It relieves premenstrual and menstrual pains

It helps to manage endometriosis

It prolongs and preserves the life of the wife and mother

It gives room to quality nursing and mother care

There are many birth control methods available. You need to see a gynecologist to know which one is the best for you. Each method has its own possible side effects – the use of birth control pills, medical surgery, or the practice of natural, non-chemical ways.

Barrier Methods – use of male and female condoms to block sperms from entering into the vagina. Others are spermicide –filled diaphragms and vaginal sponges.

Intrauterine devices (IUD's) – prevent ovulation – does not permit the ovaries to release eggs for fertilization.

Hormonal Methods – will also prevent ovulation like the Pills, Nuva Ring and injection of estrogen and progestogens into the body.

Sterilization – tubal ligation – tube cut and blocked to prevent fertilization in women; and a vasectomy for men, also blocking the tube that carries sperm.

Fertility Awareness – called natural family planning. This is done by calendar charting- monitoring days of the month in which ovulation takes place, and monitoring cervical mucus for sign of ovulation. Increase in body temperature can indicate fertile days as well, therefore coitus is avoided during these periods.

Family planning or birth control is recommended for Christians. Failure to plan is planning to fail - For which of you, intending to build a tower, sitteth not down first, and counteth the cost, whether he have sufficient to finish it? Luke 14:28. Family planing is part of counting the cost of child bearing and parenting. It is no longer how many you are able to produce but how many you can properly and adequately take or provide for - 1 Timothy 5:8, KJV: "But if any provide not for his own, and especially for those of his own house, he hath denied the faith, and is worse than an infidel."

QUESTION 82

CAN CHRISTIANS EMPLOY MEDICAL MEASURES TO ENHANCE

SEXUAL RELATIONSHIP IN MARRIAGE?

God is interested in the condition of our health; and He wants us to prosper and be in good health physically, emotionally even as our soul prosper spiritually - Beloved, I wish above all things that thou mayest prosper and be in health, even as thy soul prospereth" 3 John 1:2. It is the will of God that husband and wife should enjoy each other sexually. The use of medication to help with sexual dysfunction is not out of place in marriage. The motive behind employing medical help to boost performance should be to enhance sexual performance for the pleasure of the spouse, to enable you fulfil your sole responsibility as a husband, and not just for personal pleasure.

A husband may want to take medically recommended drugs to enable him fulfil his loving marital duty to his wife and meet her emotional needs. A wife may also take some medications and some measures to be more sexually attractive, including losing weight, keeping good personal hygiene and reducing work load in the afternoon to be able to satisfy the sexual needs of the husband whenever he desires sex. Husband and wife should help each other to be the best for each other; and enable each other to perform their roles and responsibilities well in the family.

A change in life style, eating well – balance diet, sleeping well and doing exercise may also help husband

and wife, boosting their energy for sexual performance, for mutual satisfaction. Whatever you can do possibly to serve or satisfy your spouse, and to enhance your intimacy, do it with all your heart. As you serve your spouse, it is the Lord you are serving. The Lord will not forget your labor of love and selflessness.

"And whatsoever ye do, do it heartily, as to the Lord, and not unto men; knowing that of the Lord ye shall receive the reward of the inheritance: for ye serve the Lord Christ." Colossians 3:23-24

QUESTION 83

IS ORAL SEX PERMISSIBLE FOR HUSBAND AND WIFE?

We have been talking about sex as the gift of God to the married. Husbands and wives are supposed to give pleasurable sexual experiences to each other. When it comes to oral sex, there is no Bible verse in the Old Testament and the New Testament that forbids the practice of oral sex, just as there is no verse of the Bible forbidding smoking. Though it is well known that smoking is injurious to the health of smokers, the threat of lung cancer has not stopped smokers from indulging in it. The issue is, you can choose to do what you like, but you should also be prepared to face the consequences.

The Bible says in 1 Corinthians 10:23 "All things are lawful for me, but all things are not expedient: all things are lawful for me, but all things edify not" Even if all things were lawful, not everything should be done, and nothing should be allowed to enslave us as a sinful habit. Oral sex. Anal sex, Masturbation, pornography are activities that are not edifying. They are those things which are not really convenient. They are nothing but the manifestations of reprobate minds. They are unclean sexual styles borne out the lusts of the flesh, of eyes and hearts, meant to dishonor their own bodies between themselves. The reprobate mind is really a problem. It is the cause of all the troubles in the world. It lies in the bottom of every war, every marriage break-up, every quarrel, every fight, every discord, every controversy, and tension in the church.

God is the first and the greatest fashion designer, excellent sculptor of the divine order. He created us male and female. In the act of sex, He fashioned the divine rod of the man (Penis) to fit neatly into the sacred hole of the woman (vagina) on marital bed. The rod is not just simply for the mouth. The tongue is for kissing the mouth and was not originally designed for leaking or lapping like a dog. Oral sex, sometimes referred to as oral intercourse, is sexual activity involving the stimulation of the genitalia of a wife by her husband using the mouth and the throat. Cunnilingus is oral sex performed on the vulva or vagina of the wife, while fellatio is oral sex performed on the penis of the husband.

The use of the mouth or tongue to stimulate a spouse's genitals is a perversion – twisting something from the normal, natural original use. In the love story of the Shulamite woman and her shepherd lover boy in Songs of Solomon – we hear about kissing with the mouth, of being satisfied with touching and caressing of the body and the breast, never about using the mouth on the genitals. Oral sex is not healthy, it is dangerous in the presence of all types of infections and sexually transmitted diseases. Husband and wife should read about sexual styles or different posture they can take in order for the rod to enter into the hole for mutually enjoyed sexual ecstasy. Varieties of postures add spices to sexual life. Be naturally romantic but don't go sodomy. Oral sex is not expedient for children of God, and should not be named among us.

RELATIONSHIP WITH OTHERS IN THE FAMILY

QUESTION 84

WHY ARE HOUSEMAIDS CALLED NECCESARY EVILS?

A housemaid is a male or most of the female servant employed to help in doing domestic work at home. The need to hire domestic servants for house chores, such as cleaning the house, cooking food, washing clothes, taking care of the children and others has risen as more women started working to make money and add to the family income. The role of housemaids to a busy couple cannot be over-emphasized as it help the couples, especially the working mother to be focused at work. In the days of old, women hardly worked outside the home. They were mostly housewives who stayed home to cater to the needs of their families while the husband was solely responsible for providing for the family. But these days, the reverse is the case as both men and women now share the responsibility of providing for the family. When the husband and wife are both working, someone would have to take care of the children, therefore the need for a maid arises.

Many people are against hiring of house maids because of the rise in the number of cases of child abuse committed by housemaids. Many maids have been known to commit atrocities. They can steal, serve as informants to armed robbers, and may hand you or your children over to kidnappers or hired killers. A house maid may be a satanic agent, though innocent looking. She may be demon possessed and as a result of this, serve as a point of contact through which the whole family can be opened up for satanic attacks and witchcraft manipulations in your marriage, business, ministry and health wise.

A demonic maid can initiate your innocent child into demonic world, making the children to be stealing, fighting, unruly and disobedient. Demon possessed housemaid can be manipulative, and can cause frequent quarrels between the husband and wife. We have seen a situation whereby the housemaid made the husband to sleep with her, impregnated her and sent the real wife packing. Some families though not scattered, are battling with the evil consequences of the marital bed having been defiled by housemaids. So we can see that as important as they may be, you must be very careful and watchful with housemaids. Family destroying havocs have been wrecked in some families by housemaids. If you have to employ a maid you have to be very prayerful and watchful at all times. Don't be too dependent on a maid, many have betrayed the trust put I them at the least expected moment.

Husband and wife must be very careful in bringing a housemaid to their home. Every parent should create time to care for their children personally, with or without housemaid. Some parents whose children were girls only often employ female housemaid and female lesson teachers to avoid sexual abuse. Little did they know that most of this female housemaids are also abusing the girls sexually by introducing them into lesbianism. While male housemaid and lesson teachers also introduce male Children to homosexuals.

Due to circumstances beyond control, some families cannot just do without house maids but before you employ any maid, pray very well, carry out thorough investigations and if possible demand for references. Before bringing anyone into your, home find out where the person lives, the person's family and every little information you can get. As soon as she arrives, minister salvation through Christ and deliverance to her because of her background and the baggage she may be bringing into your home. Treat your housemaid as a human being. You needed her help because you cannot do all the work in the house, therefore don't make her do all the work as well. Be firmed but don't be too harsh with them.

I am not at home with those who mal - treat house maids and use them anyhow. Treat your house maid well and you will gain a daughter or a son. By the grace of God all the housemaids I have ever had were treated like sons and daughters. To the glory of God I still have one of them with me up till now, since 2003. He is no longer our housemaid, but while under our roof, he got married, built his own house, have his own car and have gotten his own children. But right now he is still a big brother to my children, and a present help anytime I need him to help or work for me. He was a very good helper, hardworking and God- fearing. He is still part of our family till tomorrow. So, not all housemaids are demonic agents, husbands' trappers or snatchers. May God help us. Hear the word of God in

Proverbs 29:21-"He that delicately bringeth up his servant from a child shall have him become his son at the length`'". This is very true.

Having a housemaid doesn't mean you should leave her with the responsibility of training your children for you. No matter how busy or tight your schedule is, you should make out time for your husband, your children, and monitor the housemaid. Many children's destiny have been truncated, some children have been sexually abused, many have suffered damaging physical abuses, and given wrong training because they were left in the care of house maids. If you must have a maid ask the Lord to help you get the one that will be a blessing and not a source of sorrow and regrets to your family –

"Be anxious for nothing, but in everything by prayer and supplication, with thanksgiving, let your requests be made known to God; and the peace of God, which surpasses all understanding, will guard your hearts and minds through Christ Jesus" Philippians 4: 6-7. Amen.

QUESTION 85
MY WIFE CORRECTS ME IN ANGER. SHE IS VERY DISRESPECTFUL WHEN SHE IS ANGRY AND CAN SAY THINGS THAT

CHRISTIANS SHOULD NOT SAY, WHY?

As a husband or wife, no matter how provoked, should obey the word of God – "Let no corrupt communication proceed out of your mouth, but that which is good to the use of edifying, that it may minister grace unto the hearers" Ephesians 4:29. It is not proper for a wife to throw all Christian etiquette out of the window and just follow her anger and bitterness into talking carelessly and behaving disrespectfully towards her husband. A continual dropping in a very rainy day and a contentious woman are alike.

A woman has the right to be angry when wronged, but the Bible cautioned us to be angry and not sin in our anger. The Bible says it is better to dwell at the corner of a roof, than to dwell with an angry, bitter, nagging and contentious woman in a big house - contentious woman - "It is better to dwell in the corner of the housetop, than to share a house with a contentious woman" Proverbs 21:9. Such a wife should confess and repent of sin of rebellion to God, apologize to her husband and desists from talking anyhow under any circumstance.

In Ephesians 5:33, Paul writes, "let each one of you in particular so love his own wife as himself, and let the wife see that she respects her husband." Whatever happens a wife should taste her words before dishing it out. Pray for the grace to open your mouth with wisdom. The husband should examine himself and see if he himself treats his wife with respect. This is seen by the way you talk to her also. People usually respond to those who treat them with respect and decency, with an equal or even more doses of respect. Respect begets respect while contempt begets contempt. The husband should find a conducive time and raise the issue with his wife. All relational problems underneath should be resolved between the husband and wife and they should learn to forgive one another.

As the head of the wife, the husband must show leadership in the way he speaks to his wife. As he shows this example, his wife will learn from it and she is bound to speak well and with respect to him. Remember the golden rule - Do unto others as you would have them do unto you, is a biblical concept spoken by Jesus in - Luke 6:31-"And as ye would that men should do to you, do ye also to them likewise. Also, "A soft answer turneth away wrath: but grievous words stir up anger. 2 The tongue of the wise useth knowledge aright: but the mouth of fools poureth out foolishness". Proverbs 15: 1-2.

QUESTION 86
WHY CAN'T MY HUSBAND AND I COMMUNICATE WELL?

Communication is simply the act of passing information from one person or group to another. The information is sent by the sender through a communication channel to the receiver. The transmission of the message from sender to recipient can be affected by a lot of things like our emotions, cultural situation, the medium used to communicate, the person we are communication with and even the gender of the people involved and the location or the background from where the message is sent.

We can communicate in many different ways – spoken or verbal communication which includes face- to –face, telephone, radio, television, and other media. We can also communicate non- verbally, using body language – gestures, hand signals, how we stand and even the tone of our voices can give clues to the way we feel, our mood and emotional state as we communicate. Communication can also be in written form, which includes letters, e-mails, books, magazine, internet, text messages and online information. Visually, road signs, maps, logos, graphs and charts can also communicate messages.

Effective communication is the desired outcome or goal of any communication process, that it, for the receiver to receive and understand what the sender is saying. Effective communication involves active speaking, listening and responding to a message. So it is not just speaking, you need to take care that what you intent to say is exactly what is passed on, correctly understood and interpreted by the receiver accordingly. Lack of communication or ineffective communication is one of the major problems in marriage.

Many couples have difficulties in communicating, and a lot have poor communication skills. It is very important that couples communicate clearly and openly with each other to reduce conflicts, resolves problems, build intimacy and enjoy long lasting friendship in their marriage.

When a couple hardly communicates or have problem in understanding each other whenever they do, it show they have poor or bad communication skills. Following are some signs that you have ineffective or poor communication skills as a couple:-

One way communication - when a spouse is the only one talking and the other keeps silent with no response or stone walling. The problem may be one person is talking too much. Good communication should be two ways, when you speak, try and listen in a way that invites conversation, don't present your ideas as final, give room to the other person as well.

When communication becomes so official and you give directives "You have to"; "You must…" "You have not…" "You will…" The tendency for the hearer is to be defensive, and response will be negative. Communicate in a friendly, involving manner with each other.

When communication is mostly negative – if your first reaction is to shoot down the idea of your spouse and your response is always "NO" "That is not possible"

It will hinder your progress as a family. Before saying "No", listen and be considerate. Always think about solution, not objection. Be open minded enough to consider the views of your spouse without rejection always

Getting personal - focusing on people rather than problem. Don't dismiss ideas because it is coming from your spouse. Instead of getting angry or belittling your spouse, consider what is being said first and find possible way out. There is no way a negative approach to a person's view will get you good result. Where there is a will, there is always a way.

Disregarding or invalidating feelings – I don't care attitude. "That's your own problem" you are no longer concerned with the feelings or emotions of the other. It is always better to be concerned about the feelings of each other, even when you disagree. Showing that you understand their feelings and that you care, can make your spouse to be receptive to constructive criticism. Make correction in love.

When communication becomes passive aggressiveness and sarcastic – Belittling each other will block peaceful discussion, you shout and yell at each other. Most of the time your statements are sarcastic "Are you not supposed to…" "You should have known that…"using sarcasm or passive – aggression is often seen as a personal attack, it can escalate conflict and may hinder resolution.

Effective communication is more than just making your spouse get your own points of view. It is the ability to convey information to another person effectively and efficiently. You should learn to listen actively, pay attention to each other and consider each other's view without any bias.

Effective communication can be achieved by doing the following:-

Establish and maintain eye contact when you are communicating

Don't expect the other person to read your mind, you need to speak

Say exactly what you want, send a clear message

Listen carefully, be receptive and respective

Take note of non- verbal signals – tone of voice, facial expression, posture and gestures

Don't do all the talking alone. Let the other person also speak.

Wait for the other person to finish before you speak, don't interrupt

Pray that God will remove all communication barriers between you and your spouse, and that you may understand each other always

Effective communication:-

Builds trust

It reduces conflicts and results in a better understanding among husband and wife

It eliminates misunderstanding

Prevents and resolves problems

Encourages involvement or participation in family matters, makes room for direction and progress

Creates better, non-official, friendly relationship at home

Improves physical intimacy and deepens emotional intimacy

Encourages cooperation or interdependent at home

It promotes empathy and respect for each other in the family.

QUESTION 87

MY HUSBAND IS SO SELFISH? DO I HAVE ANY RIGHT TO

RECEIVE MONEY FROM HIM WHEN IN NEED?

By the grace of God, a wife has the spiritual, moral, and legal right to secure basic amenities and comfort – food, clothes, residence, education and medical treatment for herself and her children from her husband, the head of the family. A husband is bound by marital vows and responsibility to give money to his wife when she asks from him and to provide for her basic needs. In your position as a wife, you can benefit from the wealth and riches God has bestowed upon your husband. However, you need to be humble and have the right attitude of gratitude to really enjoy such benefits. You need to ask, and may be explain what you want to do with the money. Husband and wife must be accountable to each other and share whatever they have in love. It is said that you can give without love, but there is no way you will love and not give. Love gives and is always active. That is why the Bible says –

"But whoso hath this world's good, and seeth his brother have need, and shutteth up his bowels of compassion from him, how dwelleth the love of God in him? My little children, let us not love in word, neither in tongue,

but in deed and in truth" I John 3: 17 -18.

Having a selfish husband is a reality. Selfishness is not something abnormal, we are all selfish at some points in our lives, at times it is a kind of self defence. Some husbands are inherently selfish. They have the tendency to look out for themselves first in everything. In marriage relationship when the other person only takes and never gives back, life becomes suffocating and one feels trapped and frustrated. If care is not taken, confrontations and conflicts will be the order of the day in such a home.

Unfortunately, some men have stereotyped mindsets due to their upbringing and surrounding cultural background. Such men always want to have upper hand in everything and fight to have a superior, egoistic position in all things. They simply cannot tolerate when wives are well educated and are innovative, versatile or are flourishing in their career. This results in their narcissistic attitude and give rise to an inferiority complex that causes them to be mean, self-centered and cruel instead of being loving, selfless and kind. Selfishness at home manifests in many ways. These are some signs of a selfish husband that cannot be hidden at home:-

He doesn't take interest in your own interest, dreams and aspirations

Everything is his own – "My work" "My money" "My car" "My position" "In my capacity as…" My, My, My, My!

He is very generous towards himself and his courses but very stingy towards the wife. He satisfies his financial needs instantly and purposely, but that of the wife could be denied, delayed or postponed

He does not listen patiently to you, he rarely pays attention to you when you are speaking to him but he expects you to listen attentively to him when he speaks

He is always the boss, every step must begin with him and end with him, he is at the center of everything and everything must be done in his own way.

He wants to be seen and recognized to be in control, he is always in charge. He holds himself in high regard; and has extremely high self-esteem, but looks down on the wife and others, their education, position and achievement notwithstanding.

He know everything and has answers to all questions about you as a wife; and he expects you to submit totally to his ideas even when it is clear that he is wrong

He is egoistic, proud and boastful, but he relegates others, he believes other have nothing to show or tell him

He is always preoccupied with his thoughts, plans and interest – what he has done, what he is doing and what he is about to do

He is only concerned about what his needs are even when it comes to sexual life. He must be helped to do what he is supposed to do as a husband

As a husband, he has the right to be properly taken care of and be served by the wife, even when he is failing to meet the emotional needs of the wife

He is self-righteous, always criticizes, he always have a better way of doing things

He doesn't compliment the wife but very generous in complimenting others wives

He dominates every conversation, reasons out and explains every situation, and he talks too much

He is very offensive, he quickly tells you how a wife should talk and behave, and meanwhile he does the least of what is expected of a husband.

He is a king without a queen. A lion without a lioness. He is the only king in his palace, all other including the wife are subjects

He is very controlling and manipulative. He always find a way to blame the wife for any conflict, he is always right and the wife is always wrong

A narcissistic person, always wants to be on the winning side, he does not care or think about how his actions have affected his wife because after all, a wife, is expected to submit to her husband in all things.

Should these be said about a Christian husband or wife? No sir. No ma. These characteristic qualities are contrary to the Christian charter as illustrated in I Corinthians Chapter 13 on love. The opposite of love is not hatred, it is selfishness. Such a husband is disobedient to the law of God that says husband should love their wives selflessly-

"Husbands, love your wives and do not be bitter against them".

Colossians 3:19

"Husbands love your wives, even as Christ also loved the church and gave himself for it…so ought men to love their wives as their own bodies.

He that loveth his wife loveth himself" Ephesians 5: 25 - 28.

Selfish husband and wife need to confess their sin of self- centeredness, dethrone self and let God have His ways in their lives and family. Whatever you are, wherever you may be, whatever you may have is given. It is not of him that runneth or of him worketh but of God that showeth mercy.

"For who maketh thee to differ from one another?

And what hast thou, which thou didst not received? Now if thou didst receive it, why dost thou glory, as if thou did not receive it" I Corinthians 4:7."John answered and said, a man can receive nothing,

except it be given him from heaven" John 3:27.

The Bible says what God has joined together, let no man put asunder. Nothing should divide or separate husband and wife – not money, power, position or education. All these are ephemeral and time bound. The bond of unity in marriage is such that a husband and wife in oneness and in togetherness can share their lives, joy, challenges and sorrows. Let us remove selfishness, be like Christ and love each other with Agape, the unconditional love of God. And le the wife see that she respect her husband.

QUESTION 88
MY WIFE IS DOMINEERING, WHY MUST SHE HAVE HER WAY ALL THE TIME?

Dominion is defined as control or power over, or authority to rule over someone or something. The Lord God Almighty is the creator, the sovereign of the universe and the chief executive manager of all that He has created. God is omnipresent, omniscient and omnipotent. This means God is not limited by time and space, He is everywhere, He knows all things and He can do all things. At creation, God said "Let us make man in our image , after our likeness, and let them have dominion over the fish of the sea, ... So God created man in his own image, in the image of God created he him, male and female created he them. And God bless them, and God said to them, Be fruitful, and multiply, and replenish the earth, and subdue it: and have dominion...upon the earth" Genesis 1: 25 -28.

In this context, what does it mean to have dominion? It is to be productive, to manage well the resources of the earth. It means under God, humanity has responsibility to take care of the earth, making it productive in the best way possible to the glory of God. When it comes to the family affairs God gave the man – the husband the authority to manage, to coordinate the affairs of the family and make sure the wife especially is productive and be her best under the authority or leadership of her husband in the family. Even after the fall of man as a result of sin, God still emphasized the fact that wives should look up to their husband for directives, that the husband should lead, guide and make the best out of their wives

"Unto the woman he said, I will greatly multiply thy sorrow and thy conception; in sorrow you shall bring forth children; and thy desire shall be to thy husband, and he shall rule over thee: Genesis 3:16.

It takes the grace of God to be humble. For a wife to be domineering therefore, is to challenge the ruling authority God has given to her husband over her, before and after the fall. A wife is not given the permission to lord it over her husband. She is to submit to the authority, the leadership and guardian of her husband at home. This not to say that she cannot express herself or contribute to decision making in the family. It is her duty because of her role as a wife to help, to advice, to suggest and to reason with her husband on how things could be done in the best way possible in the family. For a woman to want to have things done her way in the family, is not proper. It is a sign of selfishness, self-centeredness, and sometimes a manifestation of witchcraft manipulation. A wife should allow the husband – the head of the family to be in charge, and to have the final say in family matters. A wife should always pray for the grace to recognize, accept and submit to the husband's authority at home,

However, it is good to know that God created us as single individuals. He gave us natural instinct, an inborn trait called temperament. This natural way of doing things could influence the way people act and do things. That is why we need to study Temperament, we need to understand the reason why our spouses behave the way they do. Temperament is an individual's characteristics level of expressing emotion which is typically recognized within the first few weeks after birth. It is often assumed to be an early indication of personality, which combines temperament with experiences to shape life-long traits.

There are five basic temperaments types, these are:-

Sanguine – warm, active, enthusiastic, highly talkative, extroverted and social.

Choleric – independent, decisive, goal-oriented, domineering, hot, and fast

Melancholic – calm, analytical, detailed –oriented, deep thinker, wise and quiet

Phlegmatic – cool, relaxed, peaceful, easy going and calculative

Supine –quiet, service – oriented, servant-leader, Selfless and dependable,

A domineering wife is a choleric woman in temperament - a take-charge woman. She is very energetic, outgoing and is always up to something new. She is courageous and determined, she believes she can do whatever she sets her mind to do. She is not intimidated by obstacles, she uses obstacles as stepping stones to get her goals. She could be bossy, overly aggressive and domineering. She is often considered a threat by men, resented and judged by other women who tend to want to cut her down to size.

Since the choleric woman is so hard-working, goal-oriented and energetic, she tends to lead an exceptionally productive life. She is not a stay at home woman, she craves more than just being a wife and mother. Because of her need to be productive, she is independent, authoritative and likes to be in charge. She is impulsive, impatient, and she takes strong actions to get the results she wants. She uses people and does not take time to make friends. She is a workaholic. She works beyond working hours and uses her energy for what she deems important.

Husbands of choleric wives should understand the nature of their energetic, goal-oriented and independent wives, to be able to enjoy their God-given traits. Their husbands should help them to work on their weaknesses and make correction in love. Most husbands of choleric wives tend to resent the tendency of the wives to be in charge, and often oppose the ideas of their wives in protest. They question the authority of their choleric wives taking certain decisions without consulting them.

They are not comfortable with the self-sufficient and independent life-style of their wives. These may be the reasons why they see their wives as domineering and wanting to have their ways in everything. In any case, a wife should submit to the authority of the husband. The husband should also understand the wife, encourage and support her to be her best to the glory of God.

CONFLICT MANAGEMENT IN THE FAMILY
AND RELATIONSHIP WITH IN-LAWS
QUSTION 89

MY WIFE AND I, WHY ARE WE ALWAYS IN CONFLICT?

Conflict is a serious disagreement or argument, a struggle between two people which may be physical or between conflicting ideas. We often hear that "Conflict is as old as man"; Conflict is a normal part of life. But conflict, dispute, or quarrel doesn't just happen. There are reasons why people fight or disagree with each other, whether it is at home, work, play, or at school. Knowing the reason for a dispute makes reconciliation easier.

Conflicts or quarrels occur as a complex of needs intertwined with relationship obligations or responsibilities. Conflicts are common between couples. There are many problems that could cause conflicts between a husband and wife. These include:-

Relationship factor – family or marital relationship is supposed to be the best, mutually enjoyable and satisfactory of all human relationships. Husband and wife are supposed to relate cordially well and be friendly with each other. A strained relationship where there is no more expression of love, joy, laughter and satisfaction is like a keg of gun powder that will explode with a little provocation. Take care of your relationship, nurture it very well and let it blossom. Relationship help to keep us alive.

Unmet needs – conflict always occur when basic human needs are not met either physically, spiritually, emotionally, psychologically and financially. Supplying one and denying any could lead to revolt and quarrels. No man is really sufficient to meet all the needs of a spouse, but our sufficiency is of God.

Misunderstanding – about differences in the nature of man and woman, differences in roles and responsibilities, differences in level of expectations, differences in values, needs and priorities could cause conflict about what? and How? Things should be done at home.

Poor communication – Effective communication in quantity and quality is very important in marriage relationship. Effective communication depends on clear and complete messages being sent as well as being received and rightly understood. Take time to discuss, and listen to each other. Poor communication leads to distancing – physically and emotionally. It gives room to suspicion, assumption and sorts of imaginations.

Emotional baggage- A spouse's past experience may affect the perception and articulation of their complaints. Emotions are powerful and could be the driving force in a conflict. Feelings of anger, and fear are believed to be the major drivers in conflicts. Ignoring one's emotions, or the emotions of others, can be a blockage to conflict resolution.

Values - Values explain what "good" bad is "Right" or "wrong", "just" and "unjust". Value conflicts are caused by perceived or actual incompatible belief systems. Ethnic or cultural life, educational level, religious belief and social status determine value. Frustration, anger and bitterness set in when values are not recognized, accepted or appreciated. This is essentially why inter-ethnic marriage face more challenges.

Spiritual or demonic attacks - In this life, our conflicts are not only physical and emotional, they are also spiritual. A family could be under demonic or satanic attack. Quarrels and misunderstanding in the family could originate from the spiritual realm before they manifest in constant fighting, bickering, lack of peace and joy in the family. The bible has hinted us on this - "For we wrestle not against flesh and blood, but against principalities, against powers, against the rulers of the darkness of this world, against spiritual wickedness in high places. 13 Wherefore take unto you the whole armor of God, that ye may be able to withstand in the evil day, and having done all, to stand" Ephesians 6:12-13.

Jesus Christ our Lord has fought the battle against principalities and powers, made a public show of them and defeated them. Any family under attack should never fear, but have faith in God. Pray and use the authority of the believer and the power of agreement to destroy every work of the devil over your family. No weapons sharpen against you shall prosper. We are always victorious and more than conquerors through Christ Jesus. Amen.

Conflicts are necessary and valuable for the evolution of a marriage. When conflicts are properly managed it help couples learn from each other and improve their relationships. Unresolved conflicts in marriages may produce various personal, familial, physical spiritual and psychological consequences. Conflicts should be settled as soon as they occur, The Bible encourages husband and wife to identify and settle their quarrels daily. Avoiding conflict, sweeping problems under the carpet is giving room to the devil-

Be ye angry, and sin not: let not the sun go down upon your wrath:

Neither give place to the devil" "Ephesians 4:26 -27.

QUESTION 90
HOW SHOULD A HUSBAND AND WIFE SETTLE THEIR QUARRELS?

We have heard that conflict or quarrel is part of life. Generally conflict could be with self, between a husband and wife, with environment and in the supernatural. Conflict is inevitable among families, and the ways families choose to resolve conflict makes a huge difference. Any conflict that is not solved can grow deeper or escalate in scope and bound, and that can be highly destructive. Husband and wife are likely to quarrel for many obvious reasons, but that is not the end of the story. When quarrels happened it should be settled immediately. Husband and wife who peacefully resolve their conflicts may grow closer as they learn from one another and work hard to take one another's feelings into consideration. When conflict remains unresolved, however, it may lead to family members harboring anger, growing resentful and trying to force other family members to take sides.

It is very important to resolve problems within a marriage because of the intimate nature of the relationship. It is best not to let problems fester. The Bible emphasizes the importance of reconciliation, even before any religious service – "Therefore, if you bring your gift to the altar, and there recall that your brother has anything against you, 24 leave your gift there at the altar, go first and be reconciled with your brother, and then come and offer your gift" Mathew 5:23-24.

Husband and wife should avoid taking their family problems outside of their immediate family. You don't have to let the extended family members know that you are in conflict. As children of God and lovers who have sworn to live together till death, you should be able to settle your quarrels amicably between the two of you. You need to identify or state the problem. If you know the origin or history of the conflict you are likely understand the influential factors and therefore get an effective way of finding the solution.

When there is conflict or quarrel, husband and wife should identify the problem, talk it out or discuss with each other and pray for godly solution. Husband and wife should:-

Find a good time to discuss about the problem - Talk with your spouse when both of you are well-rested and able to focus. Don't try to solve problems when one or both of you are distracted, tired, or hungry. For instance, if your spouse has just come home from work, give them some time to unwind before you bring up something that's bothering you. Early morning discussion is suggested because both of you are fresh and ready to take on another day. It is good to clear all doubts and fear before facing a new day.

Sit down and face each other – stay calm by siting down to talk instead of standing up or pacing around the room. Make eye contact with your spouse to show that you are listening attentively. It also helps you to feel more connected to each other.

Discuss the problem with your spouse – Tell your spouse exactly what is bothering you. Speak calmly, avoid pointing fingers, and don't throw accusations at your spouse. These will make him or her feel defensive, and your argument could turn into a full- blown fight. Instead, say how you feel, and what you thing. Avoid blame shifting and the use of negative words such as "never" and "always".

Keep your cool. Don't raise your voice, call your spouse names, or get sarcastic. Acting nasty will put a stop to any productive discussion you might have had. If you feel your temper rising, call a time-out and regain your composure before continuing.

Focus on the issue at hand. Argue about one thing at a time. Don't drag unrelated issues or old grudges into the conversation. Leave the past where it belongs – behind you. If you've already forgiven your spouse for something, don't dredge it up again.

Listen attentively - Listen actively to your spouse. Keep an open mind as you listen and pay attention to non- verbal gestures as well as the words used. Make sure you understand what your spouse is saying by asking clarifying questions.

Stay civil and polite. Some things, like name-calling – "Stupid" "idiot" "fool" or picking at your spouse's insecurities, should remain off-limits during an argument. If you're angry enough that you want to say something to hurt your spouse, step away and cool down by yourself. Don't just talk, open your mouth with wisdom- Mathew 12.38 "But I say to you, that every idle word that men shall speak, they shall give account thereof in the day of judgment".

Don't assume or jump to conclusions. Give your spouse the benefit of the doubt. Don't put words in their mouth or look for reasons to assume the worst. Make sure you understand what they're saying before you answer them.

Avoid trying to win every argument. Choose happiness over being right. We all want to win arguments, but needing to defeat the other person all the time will destroy your relationship. If you're arguing about something trivial, or if you think you really might be wrong, let your spouse win

You may decide to give in, Compromise or Collaborate - Giving in or accommodating the other spouse requires a lot of cooperation and little courage, this might be viewed as letting the other have his way. Compromise requires both courage and consideration, husband and wife should look for common ground, and consider each other's view and feelings. Agree on major issues and let go of smaller ones. Collaboration requires great courage and much consideration. It involves listening t discussing areas of agreement and ensure that both know what they are doing. This is resolving conflict without concessions.

Be reconciled –To be reconciled is to restore friendly, cordial relation between a husband and wife. It is to settle the quarrel, to restore harmony and to bring back peace into the relationship of husband and wife. No matter the problem, it is good for husband and wife to be reconciled.

Forgive and forget – Forgiveness is a conscious, deliberate decision to release feelings of resentment or vengeance toward a person who has hurt or harmed you, regardless of whether they actually deserve it. It releasing the other spouse from blame, leaving the event in God's hands and moving on. To forget is to deliberately cease to think of, to stop thinking about something, to ignore, to overlook and put out of one's mind. Children of God are commanded to forgive each one another –

Colossians 3:13. 13 Bear with each other and forgive one another if any of you has a grievance against someone. Forgive as the Lord forgave you.

Matthew 6:14-15. 14 For if you forgive other people when they sin against you, your heavenly Father will also forgive you. ...

Luke 17:3-4. 3 So watch yourselves. "If your brother or sister sins against you, rebuke them; and if they repent, forgive them.

If it ever happens that both of you have avoided conflict and now you are both boiling with anger and resentment, and it seems you cannot handle the conflict by yourselves, please go for counseling. When discussing the problem among husband and wife alone is getting difficult, when you always raise your voices and say bad things to each other at every attempt you made to discuss your problems – you both need counseling. Even if a spouse does not wish to go for counseling, the other one should go to save the relationship from totally breaking down. Prevention is always better than cure. Mathew 18: 14- 17.

"Moreover if thy brother shall trespass against thee, go and tell him his fault between thee and him alone: if he shall hear thee, thou hast gained thy brother. 16But if he will not hear thee, then take with thee one or two more, that in the mouth of two or three witnesses every word may be established. "And it he shall neglect to hear them, tell it to the church…" (Counseling unit)

To avoid future conflict, husband and wife should not pick at each other for little things. Don't live a cat and mouse life - of constant watching out to pin point the mistake of the other. Learn to distinguish between real problems and minor issues you can ignore. Appreciate each other and focus on good traits, and be generous about complimenting each other sincerely well. Always say "Thank you" when your spouse does something thoughtful for you. Let your spouse make mistakes, because no one is perfect. Your spouse will make mistakes just like you would do too. Spend quality time together all the time. Make a habit of going out together and doing many things together. Pray for each other every day, every time, and everywhere.

QUESTION 91
MY HUSBAND LISTENS TO HER MOTHER MORE THAN HIS WIFE, WHY SHOULD THIS BE?

When God ordained marriage he laid down the principle of relationship with in-laws, emphasizing the prominence of the marriage relationship over any other relationships before or after it. "And Adam said, This is now bone of my bones, and flesh of my flesh: she shall be called Woman, because she was taken out of Man. 24 Therefore shall a man leave his father and his mother, and shall cleave unto his wife: and they shall be one flesh." Genesis 2: 23 -24.

Husband and wife are two individuals who have become a single entity by the virtue of their marriage. If the two are going to walk and work together, enjoy their union, they must "leave" and "Cleave". Marriage implies that two of you will set aside your parents, siblings and other relatives aside, and focus on the new relationship as husband and wife. Leaving does not mean that you have to abandon your parents, siblings and others, but they are no longer the first people to be considered in your life.

Husband and wife should understand that the parenting relationship is the only relationship designed by God to come to an end. God never intended for parents to continue giving instructions and guidance to their adult child. When children become independent adults, it means that they are no longer dependent on their parents emotionally, financially, or intellectually. They are to act and think separately and apart from their parents.

Before marriage your parents could be so loving and caring that leaving them physically and emotionally may be difficult but you still have to.

It may be that yours parents are so domineering and authoritarian that you get permission before doing anything, and they have the last say on everything about you, but now you should realize that your status has changed. You are now a husband or wife, by the virtue of your marriage you have a special title of being a husband and a wife. Your parents have no right to control, dictates and instruct you what and how to manage your marital affairs. You have left them, you are no longer under their authority, and you yourself have become an authority in your home.

A husband who has his mother as a confidant and who has all airs for his mother beside that of his wife is disobedient to the injunction of God to leave his parents and Cleave to his wife. If husbands and wives wants peace and enduring love in their marriage, they must learn how to leave their parents. The new number one in your life now is your spouse, and is your next of kin. You should seek advice from your wife not your mother, from your husband and not your father, no matter how close you may have been before marriage. You must adjust to your new marital relationship with your wife.

Husband and wife must depart physically and emotionally from their parents and siblings because of the potential stress, anxiety and hurt that can result from not doing so. You are not expected to break off completely with your parents and former family members it is just that their own status has changed too, they are now in-laws. You should never stop honoring your parents, calling them and visiting them occasionally but all they have to do is to pray for you and let you be what marriage has made you to be – a husband and wife, no longer son and daughter. Your allegiance now is towards your spouse and no longer your parents.

Here are some ways couples fail to leave their parents, if any of these apply to your marriage, please take necessary step to correct yourself – leave your parents and cleave to your wife or husband.

Parental wealth and social benefits – This problem reveals dependence on parents for financial or social benefits to the point that the couple fails to acknowledge their own independence. Some are still living in their parents' house, this is wrong. You should never bring a wife to your family house after the wedding. You should look for a place, no matter how small to start your own family life. If possible live in a different city or state, and under no circumstances should you live on the same street or in a place very close to your family house. Problems with in- laws – physical, financial and emotional interference have destroyed many marriages.

Parental model – Some couples, again consciously or subconsciously, compare some area of their spouse's performance to that of their parents. These comparisons can especially take place in early marriage and can be very damaging. Your wife is not your mother, so don't expect to see your mother in her. She will eventually become the wife you want her to be under you tutelage and care as a husband. There is no room for comparison or unrealistic expectations.

Parental approval – Some spouses remain dependent on their parents' approval after marriage due to an extremely strong or domineering parent. The need for parental approval may block trust in their new mate. You are on your own, make your decision after discussing with your wife. You mother has no authority over your new family, she can only pray for you now.

Parental relationship substitute – Some men and women continue to call or go see their parents about most key issues in their lives, sometimes before they consult their mate. This in turn creates a lack of dependence on the spouse. Stop talking to your parents or siblings about your plan and purposes, discuss with your wife.

"If ye be willing and obedient, ye shall eat the good of the land,…" Isaiah 1:19. The word of God says if you are willing to obey God, to leave and cleave to your wife, you will eat the fruit of marriage for a long time with joy and satisfaction. Be willing to obey God, and be committed to your husband or wife. Let your spouse be your confidant and trust her enough to seek her opinion and advice instead of from parents or siblings. The peace of God beyond all human understanding will be your portion at home.

QUESTION 92

TO WHAT EXTENT SHOULD MOTHER, FATHER IN-LAW AND OTHERS IN-LAWS GET INVOLVED IN THEIR CHILDREN'S MARRIAGE?

No in-law – mother, father, sister, brother, or any other in-law should meddle in the marital affairs of husband and wife. According to God's directives, it is written:-

And he answered and said unto them, Have ye not read, that he which made them at the beginning made them male and female,

And said, for this cause shall a man leave father and mother,

and shall cleave to his wife: and they twain shall be one flesh?

Wherefore they are no more twain, but one flesh.

What therefore God hath joined together,

Let not man put asunder. Mathew 19: 4-6.

Husband and wife should leave their parents and bond to their spouse. The newlyweds are to build their own home with their own rules, traditions, and practices. They should be allowed to make mistakes and learn from their mistakes as they grow together in their newness of life without undue interference. Whenever there is interference from the outside, there is bound to be problems and confusion.

In-law problems are a reality most especially in families that are interdependent, and it is often very hard for their children to be detached from the apron spring. However, this is detrimental to newlyweds and it usually leads to troubles, trials, hurts and heartaches for husband and wife. From experience it is common to hear in a family with in-law problems complaints such as-

My in-laws are making life difficult for me as a wife

My in-laws have no respect for me and my privacy

My in-laws are clingy and overly attached to my spouse

My mother-in-law judges and criticizes my every move

My in-laws are trying to turn me and my spouse against each other

My in-laws are to sensitive and too much involved in my married life

My in-laws are very rude and unfriendly to me

My in-laws are to bossy and controlling

My in-laws are not allowing me to breath in my home

My mother – in-law is too inquisitive and poke nosing

In-laws are part of any extended family units and cannot be wished away. They must be respected, honored and cared for as much as possible. But in-laws are not in any way to become a thorn in the flesh of husband and wife. It is true that when one marries, you also become a part of another family with its own set of values and expectations. These expectations and values need to be recognized and respect within limits. Honoring in-laws does not necessarily imply that:-

You submerge all your own feelings, desires, preferences, and needs in the service of "doing things their way."

You must permit them to disrespect, control, or manipulate you for their own selfish ends.

It entails "obeying" all their "parental" requests or requirements which, in some instances with some in-laws, could be detrimental to your own personal being and your marriage.

Sometimes the most honoring response is to diplomatically but firmly say, "No." Letting in-laws split, manipulate, or control you by silently condescending to their selfish, neurotic, inappropriate expectations and demands is not necessarily showing Christian love. In-law conflicts grow more complicated when a spouse seems to side with his or her parents and against his or her mate. The other spouse may rightly feel outnumbered or "ganged up on." This is not good for the husband and wife relationship at all.

Should be now cut ourselves from our family of origin because of marriage? No! Not at all, if the in-laws are reasonable and accommodating. Maintaining relationships with our parents usually is beneficial. But problems arise if factors like the following are present:

One spouse relies too heavily on the parents to help in decision-making, leading the other spouse to feel insignificant.

One spouse looks to the parent, not the partner, to get his or her emotional needs met, leading the partner to feel ignored.

One spouse reveals details of marital conflict with his or her parents, leading the other spouse to feel betrayed.

One spouse putting the needs of parents as first making them more important to the spouse – generating the feeling of insecurity, divided loyalty and perverted love.

In a situation where parents or in-laws suspect or know that the couple are having problem. They don't just get involved just like that. They must first give the opportunity for the couple to voluntarily request their involvement in the situation. They should not intervene, nor enter their marital matters without permission. If the parent or in-law notices that the couple is in misery, pain, or deep frustration, the in-law can gingerly state what they observe and give their concern. The principle is do not force your way into the privacy of the home.

It is very possible for a couple to avoid in-laws interference, and grow as a single family unit, away from parental involvement. A couple needs to understand the autonomy of their new marital status and their need to act and think without in-law's involvement. Family problems should be settled among the husband and wife, and not to be shared with someone else. Ideally, newlyweds should live away from parents and in-laws. They should live in a different house, and if possible at a considerable distance from in-laws. A couple is not ready for marriage if they cannot afford to live separately from mom and dad.

Marriage is for well-adjusted, independent thinking, emotionally and financially mature adults, not for dependent baby-husband or wife. A couple needs to set up impregnable barriers so that inquisitive in-laws may not break through to their family affairs. They may do this by honoring and respecting for each other. By daily nurturing and caring for their relationship as husband and wife. By recognizing the fact that their relationship as husband and wife is superior above any other relationship, and by their closeness, support, and care for each other's feelings when they are with in-laws, relatives and friends.

QUESTION 93

WHAT IS PARENTING? WHICH IS THE BEST

PARENTING METHOD OR STYLE?

Parenting or child rearing is the process of promoting and supporting the physical, emotional, social, and intellectual development of a child from infancy to adulthood. Parenting refers to the intricacies of raising a child and not exclusively for a biological relationship. The most common caretaker in parenting is the father or mother, or both, biological parent of the child in question, although a surrogate may be an older sibling, a grandparent, a legal guardian, aunt, uncle or other family member for one reason or the other. God specifically gives parents instructions to train their children in the fear and admonition of the Lord:-

"Train up a child in the way he should go: and when he is old, he will not depart from it" Proverbs 22:6. "And ye fathers, provoke not your children to wrath but bring them up in the nurture and admonition of the Lord," Ephesians 6:4.

To parent effectively is, it is not just enough to simply avoid the obvious dangers like abuse, neglect, or overindulgence. Also, parents are expected to maintain their children's health and safety, promoting their emotional well-being, instilling social skills, and preparing the children to be spiritually, intellectually, socially and morally upright. Children are to be properly trained so that they may have a brighter future, be useful to themselves, their families and the societies at large. It has been proved psychologically that the best –adjusted children are brought up by parents who find a way to combine warmth and sensitivity with clear spiritual and behavioral expectations. Parents should care for their children – showing acceptance and affection, be consistent in maintaining a stable spiritual and socio-cultural environment, allow children to make choices in other to develop independent and avoid total dependency on parents; and also let the children face the consequences of their choices whether positive or negative.

Parenting styles differ from family to family, and may even vary from time to time within a family. There are four major parenting styles, namely:-

Authoritarian parenting – parents are very strict, unbending and inflexible. They attempt to control every aspect of their children's lives, and give no room for choices. Such children may not be able to act without specific instructions, and may find it difficult to express themselves.

Authoritative parenting – these parents are firm, loving and kind. They are neither overtly strict nor indulgent. Their children often display social competence, independence and high sense of responsibility as they grow into adulthood.

Permissive Parenting –Permissive parents are indulgent, not wanting to impose their will on their children's development. They neither set rules, nor discourage poor choices or bad behaviour. Such children are likely to struggle academically, exhibit moral behaviour problems and they often have low self-esteem and suffer depression.

Uninvolved / Neglectful parenting- these parents have no time to take care of their children. They are absentee parents. They expect the children to raise themselves. Children raised up in this pattern struggles with very low self-esteem, perform poorly academically and have trouble adjusting to societal rules and regulations.

For all Christians, we should pattern our parenting style on the Word of God, or Biblical principles. Biblical principles of parenting are based on the word of God according to the Bible. Children are expected to be raise according to the knowledge of the word of God – giving them instructions, correction and applying discipline when needed. According to this principle, parents are to:-

1. Live exemplary lives – what parents do before their children, the way the parents treat other people really matters. Children are learning from what their parents do.

2. Be involved in their children's lives – to be there for the children physically, mentally and spiritually. It means sacrificing what you want to do for what your children needs to do.

3. Establish and set rules - If you don't manage your children's behavior when they are young, they will have a hard time learning how to manage themselves when they are older and you are not around. Any time of the day or night, you should always be able to answer these three questions: Where is my child? Who is with my child? What is my child doing? The rules your child has learned from you are going to shape the rules he applies to himself.

4. Foster your child's independence. Setting limits helps your child develop a sense of self-control. Encouraging independence helps her develop a sense of self-direction. To be successful in life, they are going to need both.

5. Be consistent. If your rules vary from day to day in an unpredictable fashion or if you enforce them only intermittently, your child's misbehavior is your fault, not his. Your most important disciplinary tool is consistency. Identify your non-negotiables. The more your authority is based on wisdom and not on power, the less your child will challenge it.

6. Avoid harsh discipline. Parents should avoid physical and emotional abuse – hitting a child and calling him or her name "never do well" "idiot" "fool" are too morally degrading. Children who are verbally abused, hit, or

slapped are more prone to be aggressive and fight with other children. They are more likely to be bullies and more likely to use aggression to solve disputes with others. There are many other ways to discipline a child -- including 'time out' which work better and do not involve aggression.

7. Love and treat your child with respect. It is simply not possible to spoil a child with love; and the best way to get respectful treatment from your child is to treat him respectfully. Steinberg writes. You should give your child the same courtesies you would give to anyone else. Speak to him politely. Respect his opinion. Pay attention when he is speaking to you. Treat him kindly. Try to please him when you can. Children treat others the way their parents treat them. Your relationship with your child is the foundation for her relationships with others.

8. Pray for your children and with them always – God would have us pray always for and with our children without ceasing. We are not to be anxious or fear about the children but commit their ways unto the Lord every day in prayers. "Be anxious for nothing, but in everything by prayer and supplication, with thanksgiving, let your requests be made known to God. And the peace of God, which surpasses all understanding will guard your hearts and minds through Christ Jesus". Philippians 4: 6-7.

QUESTION 94

MY HUSBAND IS TOO HARSH WITH THE CHILDREN, WHAT CAN I DO?

For a parent to be harsh in this context is to be ungentle and unpleasant in action or effect with a child. Harsh verbal discipline happens when parents use force to make a child to experience emotional pain or discomfort in an effort to correct or control behavior. It can vary in severity from yelling and shouting at a child to insulting and using words to humiliate. Many parents shift from physical to verbal discipline as their children enter adolescence. The word of God however tells us not to be too harsh with our children to avoid provocation.

"And, ye fathers, provoke not your children to wrath: but bring them up in the nurture and admonition of the Lord. Ephes. 6:4.

"Fathers, provoke not your children to anger, lest they be discouraged".

Colossians 3:21.

One wonders why father are always strict or harsh with children. Most of the time it is because fathers have little time to spend with their children, they are always out looking for how to provide basic necessities for the family. However, God know about the duties of the head of the family before warning fathers in particular to take it easy with their children. Harshness, high- handedness is not too good for the children. Harsh parenting is regarded as angry, hostile and antisocial. And having one kind, caring parent – most of the time the mother, doesn't seem to counteract the effects of the harsh father.

Harsh parents Abusive can negatively affect the mental well-being of their children, by creating a toxic family environment. When parents act with hostility towards a child, the child tends to become angrier, more irritable, and more belligerent. Rather than feeling nurtured, he frequently becomes suspicious of his angry parents, feeling the need to defend himself, which often leads to bad behavior. Yelling doesn't help. Harsh verbal discipline not only isn't effective, it actually makes things worse and creates potentially long-lasting psychological problems for the children and damages parent-child relationships.

Harsh verbal discipline also increases depression due to the child's belief that they are "useless," "worthless," or "inferior," as their parents' harsh criticism might suggest. In turn, a child can become overly self-critical, experience low self-esteem, and exhibit a pattern of poor choices regarding peers and behavior. Unfortunately, being the warm parent you want to be after a verbal blowout can't undo the damage. Verbal punishment eats away at a child's willingness to trust his parent. Always pray for your children, commit their heart and their ways unto the Lord, ask God to fill them with the Holy Spirit, Who will guide them to behave well.

Parents should create quality time out of their busy schedules to be with their children. Listen to your children and be at home for them physically and emotionally. When you take time to relate with them lovingly and being kind to your children, you will have no reason to shout or yell at them. Fathers do not make your children angry with you. Avoid severity, anger, harshness, and cruelty. Impatience, harsh parents generally have bad children.

"And ye fathers, provoke not your children to wrath: but bring them up in the nurture and admonition of the Lord" Ephesians 6:4.

Correct your children in love, do not punish them. Punishment is from a principle of revenge, correction is from a principle of affectionate concern. Train your children in the nurture and admonition of the Lord. Let their mind be nourished with wholesome discipline and instruction which will bend them toward God and Christian living.

FAMILY CRISES AND HOW TO HANDLE THEM

QUESTION 95

WHAT ARE FAMILY CRISIS? HOW DO WE DEAL WITH THEM

A crisis is any event that is going to lead to an unstable and dangerous situation affecting an individual, group, community or a whole society. Crisis refers to an unexpected, unplanned situation or rather a threat that suddenly come upon a family out of nowhere. It means an event that threatens the very stability of the family. Crisis is a kind of a bolt from the blue – something that is least expected to happen – a father or the bread winner of the family is suddenly laid off from work, a child dies at a prime age, Fire outbreak that destroys all family properties, a mother diagnosed with cancer, a pregnancy that needs bedrest for the best outcome, infidelity of a spouse and appearance of a strange woman – can suddenly hit the family.

Crises are deemed to be negative changes in the security, economic, political, societal, or environmental affairs, especially when they occur abruptly, with little or no warning. A family crisis occurs when a family has to change. It is a turning point and things may never be the same in the family. Waller and Hill 1956 say crisis is something that makes one strive for a different and unusual solution of the problem. Any rupturing of family relationships which forces reorganization of the family pattern not only constitutes a family crisis but is also a threat to family unity. Crises are part of life, crisis refines, and redefines life, in them you discover you really are.

For a family of God, it is easier to deal with crisis because of the love, mercy, and grace of God. The Word of God are the great shock absorber in time of Crisis, they give assurance and encouragement that all will be well. God is our Jehovah Shama, always there for us at all time - "God is our refuge and strength, a very present help in trouble. 2 Therefore will not we fear, though the earth be removed, and though the mountains be carried into the midst of the sea" Psalm 46: 1-2. When trouble comes, every Child of God should look up for help and support because God will always be there to help us out- "For the Lord GOD will help me; therefore shall I not be confounded: therefore have I set my face like a flint, and I know that I shall not be ashamed" Isaiah 50: 7

CAUSES OF CRISIS IN THE FAMILY _ some life situations in the family that can cause crises includes:-

1. Unfaithfulness in marriage – defiling the marital bed, having sex outside marriage, adultery, and having children out of wedlock

2. Sickness – Physical and mental health crisis – discovery of terminal disease like HIV AIDS, loss of eye-sight, paralysis, stroke, malignant tumor.

Mental health disorders like anxiety, depression, panic attacks, Post traumatic disorder etc may cause untold hardships in the family.

3. Childlessness – infertility. Impotency, bareness, or delay in child bearing.

4. Sudden Prosperity –" Nouveau Riche" availability of too much money, when money begins to control people there will be careless and frivolous spending leading to all kinds of wrong doings – lies, secrecy, adultery, absenteeism, pride, egoism etc.

5. Long separation from spouse – due to high risk jobs – Airline workers, Sailors, soldiers, long – distance drivers, Politicians and celebrities - long or short travelling abroad, business trips, staying in hotel rooms without your spouse is dangerous. There are lots of "Strange women" or "senior girls and boys" - that is loose women and men outside there, who seduce and cause family men and women to fall into adultery and fornication.

6. Divorce Notice – forceful separation of husband and wife

7. Accident – Motor, fire, - loss of parts of the body, stroke, deformity, blindness, paralysis – wheel chair, invalidity etc.

8. Poverty – due to job loss, retirement, loss of property – houses, and investments; theft,   419 – loss of money through deceit

9. Domestic violence – battery, physical and verbal abuse, neglect, desertion

10. Sexual abuse – sexual assault like rape, incest, denial of sex by spouse

11. Substance Abuse - use of legal and illegal substance – e.g. alcohol, cocaine resulting in chemical or substance dependency.

12. Terrorism – Ritual killings, kidnapping, forceful eviction from home or fleeing for life, and all sorts of malevolence.

13. Old age - with its limitations and disabilities

14. Menopause – chemical in- balance, Heat waves or rashes

15. Impotence –due to old age or dysfunctional body parts

16. Death – loss of a child or a spouse due to human carelessness – homicide, suicide, road accident, fire accident, plague or virus infection, terminal diseases and old age.

QUESTION 96
WHAT ARE THE   CORRECT STEPS TO TAKE IN FAMILY CRISIS MANAGEMENT

First and foremost, you need to know that what has happened to you is not unique, it has been happening and will continue to happen in this world without end. A Yoruba adage says –"A o ri iru eleyi ri, eru l'afi n da b'oloro" - that is for someone to tell you when you have crisis that nothing of such has ever happened before it is just to scare you, or frighten you. There is nothing new under this planet earth. Whatever is happening has happened before. What has been is what will be, and what has been done is what will be done, and there is nothing new under the sun. 10 Is there a thing of which it is said, "See, this is new"? It has been already in the ages before us. Eccles. 1: 9-10.

However, it is also written - "There hath no temptation taken you but such as is common to man: but God is faithful, who will not suffer you to be tempted above that ye are able; but will with the temptation also make a way to escape, that ye may be able to bear it". I Cor. 10:13. God says - "Call upon me in the day of trouble; I will deliver you, and you shall glorify Me." Psalm 50:15

1. When it happens – do not panic, don't be too emotional. Identify the What? Where? How? And why? - Of the crisis.

2. Run to God – cry out to Him. "Come unto me, all ye that labor and are heavy laden, and I will give you rest". Mt 11:28, 28. "The Lord is my rock, and my fortress, and my deliverer; my God, my strength, in whom I will trust; my buckler, and the horn of my salvation, and my high tower. 3 I will call upon the Lord, who is worthy to be praised: so shall I be saved from mine enemies". Psalm 18: 2-4

3. Call a family meeting – Inform your children and immediate family members about the situation, let godly people rally round you to see to the problem.

4. Seek the necessary medical/ spiritual, judicial intervention or support –Call your family doctor, go to the hospital, make necessary report, get relevant medical certificate or police report.

5. Tell it to your Pastor - ask the brethren to pray for you – I Thessalonians 5:25 "Brethren Pray for us". Consecrate a fast, proclaim a solemn assembly, call on prayer warriors! Joel 1:14 - "Sanctify you a fast, call a solemn assembly, gather the elders and all the inhabitants of the land into the house of the LORD your God, and cry to the LORD"

6. In the case of adultery, divorce notice, desertion or any act of ungodliness - You may have to confront, question or query the people involved in the crisis. Don't allow your grievance to get the better part of you. Be calm but firm.

7. Prayerfully look for a way of resolving the problem – You may fast and pray for about three days to seek the face of the Lord for directions. Always resolve whatever problem in a godly manner. Take decisions and find solutions that will glorify God. Be willing to do the will of God, no matter how hard.

8. Do not talk too much. Don't take major decision when you are angry or confused. Be patient.

9. Plan, act in faith, put your plan into actions – what will you do now about the situation? Attend to immediate needs of the family.

10. Whatever the situation do not give up! Keep your eyes on God. Do not be distracted. In all these things you are still more than conqueror! Be strong in the Lord. Encourage yourself in the Lord. Let the joy of the Lord be your strength.

LESSONS OF LIFE IN TIME OF CRISIS FROM KING JEHOSHAPHAT - 2 Chronicles 20:1-24; QUEEN ESTHER – Esther Chapter 4.

They both acknowledged the fact that they were in crisis, they were in great danger and they did not deny this fact - a nation was under a serious threat - annihilation

They were helpless, they realized it would take God – divine intervention to get out of this trouble.

They gathered their people together for fasting and prayers

They were courageous, they did not allow themselves to be intimidated or overwhelmed by the crisis

They confronted their enemies with the power and strength of God.

They recognized the supremacy of God over every life situation and they were able to praise God even in danger

They had absolute faith in God, trusted in His ability to safe and deliver from all evils

Since they acknowledged and trusted God in their crisis, God honored their faith by fighting for them and destroying their enemies instead. Alleluia!

Wait prayerfully on the Lord, trust in His grace and mercy to make all thing work together for your good and that of the family. He is a faithful God, He cares, He never fails and He will prevail in your family situation in the name of Jesus.

Be strong in the Lord and be courageous. Through the love of God our Saviour all will be well. Amen.

Habakkuk 3:17-19 Amplified Bible- "17 Though the fig tree does not blossom and there is no fruit on the vines, [though] the product of the olive fails and the fields yield no food, though the flock is cut off from the fold and there are no cattle in the stalls, Yet I will rejoice in the Lord; I will exult in the [victorious] God of my salvation!"

DEATH – THE END OF MARRIAGE
QUESTION 97
WHY SHOULD A COUPLE WRITE A WILL?

A will or testament is a legal document that expresses a person's wishes as to how their property is to be distributed after their death and as to which person is to manage the property until its final distribution. Having a will is arguably one of the most important things you can do for yourself and your family. Not only can a will legally protect your spouse, children and assets, it can also spell out exactly how you would like things to be handled after you have passed on. If not you are putting your estate into the hands of the court, opportunists among envious family members, and endangering the life and future of your spouse and children.

Honestly, as children of God, we should not be careless and give room to the Devil concerning your hard earned wealth and resources. Having a will helps minimize any family fights about your estate that may arise and also determines the 'Who", what and When" of your estate or property. You don't have to be an expert in law to write a will. Contact a lawyer – especially a qualified estate planning attorney to help you ensure that your loved ones are cared for and your wishes are honored. Don't you ever say that you have nothing to leave for your family, the little you have is much for your spouse, biological and adopted children. Some of your properties can be willed to a church or Christian organization, instead of leaving it for marauders.

A couple should write a will for the following purposes:-

1. You have the life opportunity to decide how your estate will be distributed.

2. You decide who and who will share in your inheritance

3. You chose by yourself who will take care of your spouse and children after your departure in death

4. It will prevent untold hardship for your spouse and children and unnecessary battle with in-laws or family members who are looters.

5. It will minimize estate taxes because the value of what you give away to family members or charity will reduce the value of your estate when it is time to pay tax.

6. You will avoid unwarranted legal challenges. If you die intestate or without a will, someone may rise up and take your spouse and children to court, challenging their inheritance. Your family may lose the case and your estate will go to who you never imagined.

7. You can change your mind if your life circumstances change. Life changes, birth, death, divorce, separation can make you to change your will.

8. Most importantly, nobody knows tomorrow. Don't postpone what you can do today till tomorrow. Procrastination is the thief of time. No body plans or wants to die early, but people are dying. The insecurity of our societies today is so high that Psalm 91 has become a

reality in the lives of Christians. It is only those that are kept by God are saved. We live our lives one day at a time, trusting Jesus to keep us free from every evil attempt. So write your will today.

QUESTION 98
IF A HUSBAND OR WIFE DIES WHAT SHOULD BE DONE?

The Bible says - "To everything there is a season, and a time to every purpose under the heaven: A time to be born, and a time to die;" Eccles. 3: 1-2. The natural end of marital relationship comes at the death of a spouse – the vow is "Till death do us part". Death is part of the reality of life, we humans are all born to die. The only mystery about death that is beyond human knowledge is not knowing When, Where, and How death will come. But surely we were born and at a time known only to our creator we shall die. Our prayers is that since we came one by one, we will go one by one. Our death will not be due to natural disaster or virus pandemic in the name of Jesus. "And as it is appointed unto men once to die, but after this the judgment:" Hebrew 9:27

What is death? Death is simply the opposite of life. While death may be a certainty for all of us, it is not easy to determine the actual moment of a person's death. Death brings an end to life. The moment any person refuses to function biologically in the characteristics of living organism – (MR NIGER) acronym for Movement, Respiration, Nutrition, Irritability, Growth, Excretion and Reproduction, the person may be certified dead. Strong indications that a person is no longer alive includes stoppage of respiration – the person no longer breathes ;the body no longer metabolizes – no movement and no feelings; paleness due to the stoppage of blood flow - blood is life; coldness and stiffness of the limbs; and finally decomposition.

When death occurs early in the family, it is a crisis, the family may never be the same again. However, for Christians death is just a passage way to victory and glory. In Christ, though we mourn and grieve for our beloved, we should not mourn like unbelievers who have no hope – I Thessalonians 4: 13 -14. "But I do not want you to be ignorant, brethren, concerning those who have fallen asleep, lest you sorrow as others who have no hope. 14 For if we believe that Jesus died and rose again, even so God will bring with Him those who sleep in Jesus".

The Loss of a Spouse – The death of a spouse has been said to be the highest level of trauma, second to divorce. The sorrow that grips a spouse on the loss of the other can affect the living spouse very badly, it may drive such a spouse to his or her own death if the sorrow is allowed to linger. Coping with the loss of someone or something you love is one of life's biggest challenges. Often, the pain of loss can be overwhelming. A person may experience all kinds of difficult and unexpected emotions, from shock or anger to disbelief or denial, guilt and fear, depression or deep sorrow. At last one will see the light at the end of the tunnel. It is good to know though weeping may endure for the night but joy will come in the morning.

When a spouse dies do the following:-

1. Realize that all mankind are born to die, there is life in death and death is the end of life here on earth. Death brings an end to all human relationship and activities.

2. Call your children and close relatives to inform them

3. Confirm the death and the cause of the death

4. Call your pastor for prayers support and plans for burial

5. Discuss the burial – where and what to be done to make it a success – it is the final right, give your spouse a befitting burial. The burial will confirm the death and passing away of your spouse, it becomes a reality.

6. Grief or mourn like a believer. In this world, Christians don't die, they sleep in the Lord. Go through the stages of mourning with courage and the hope of seeing the person that died again in heaven. The dead in Christ shall rise at the resurrection. We will all be with the Lord Jesus to live forever in Heaven. Amen.

7. Discuss with your children about your welfare – where to stay, what to do to keep you going on with life. You may have to leave the house you were staying with your spouse before death for a while. Go to the children and stay to get accustomed to your loneliness.

8. Live, the death of a spouse should not be the end of life for you. Live to fulfill your God –given destiny. You also need to be alive for the sake of your children, grandchildren, your estate and your ministry. Live a victorious Christian life with the full hope of seeing or meeting with your spouse in heaven – though not as husband and wife anymore, but as brides of Christ. Alleluia!

"But I would not have you to be ignorant, brethren, concerning them which are asleep, that ye sorrow not, even as others which have no hope. 14 For if we believe that

Jesus died and rose again, even so them also which sleep in Jesus will God bring with him. 15 For this we say unto you by the word of the Lord, that we which are alive and remain unto the coming of the Lord shall not prevent them which are asleep. 16 For the Lord himself shall descend from heaven with a shout, with the voice of the archangel, and with the trump of God: and the dead in Christ shall rise first: 17 Then we which are alive and remain shall be caught up together with them in the clouds, to meet the Lord in the air: and so shall we ever be with the Lord". 1 Thessalonians 4:13–17

QUESTION 99
HOW SHOULD A CHRISTIAN GRIEVE OR MOURN?

Grief is the normal process of reacting to a loss. The loss may be physical such as a death, social such as divorce, or occupational such as a job. Emotional reactions of grief can include anger, guilt, anxiety, sadness, and despair. Physical reactions of grief can include sleeping problems, changes in appetite, physical problems, or illness. While the terms grief and bereavement are often used interchangeably, bereavement refers to the state of loss, and grief is the reaction to that loss. Everyone griefs differently. Some people will wear their emotions on their sleeve and be outwardly emotional. Others will experience their grief more internally, and may not cry. Grieving is a personal process that has no time limit, nor one "right" way to do it. It is not proper to judge how a person experiences his grief, because we are wonderfully but differently wired.

However the Bible tells us how a child of God should grief for a beloved one who has passed on to glory. For

Christians, death is not the end, it is a passage way to eternal life. Apostle Paul hinted that if it is only in this world that we Christians have hope, we should be pitied. We have the hope of eternal life with Christ in Heaven. Therefore, Christians should not grief like unbelievers who have no hope of eternal life with Christ. "But I do not want you to be ignorant, brethren, concerning those who have fallen asleep, lest you sorrow as others who have no hope". I Thessalonians 4:13.

Our transient life on earth is full of loss and full of grief. No sorrow is deeper than the sorrow of loss, most especially that of losing a spouse. While our loved ones have left us, they have not ceased to be. They've simply gone on ahead. Because Jesus rose again, they will rise again. Because Jesus conquered death, they will conquer death. Because Jesus lives, they too will live. And so we grieve hopefully because we are convinced we grieve only temporarily. We should encourage ourselves with this truth.

"But I would not have you to be ignorant, brethren, concerning them which are asleep, that ye sorrow not, even as others which have no hope. For if we believe that Jesus died and rose again, even so them also which sleep in Jesus will God bring with him. For this we say unto you by the word of the Lord, that we which are alive and remain unto the coming of the Lord shall not prevent them which are asleep. For the Lord himself shall descend from heaven with a shout, with the voice of the archangel, and with the trump of God: and the dead in Christ shall rise first: Then we which are alive and remain shall be caught up together with them in the clouds, to meet the Lord in the air: and so shall we ever be with the Lord. Wherefore comfort one another with these words+. 1 Thessalonians 4:13-18 KJV

THE STAGES OF GRIEF - The stages of grief or mourning are universal and are experienced by people from all walks of life, across many cultures. There are five stages of grief that were first proposed by Elisabeth Kübler-Ross in her 1969 book On Death and Dying. Others have discovered more stages than five, but they are all interwoven. The 5 stages of grief and loss are: - Shock and Denial; Anger; Bargaining; Depression; and Acceptance. People who are grieving do not necessarily go through the stages in the same order or experience all of them.

1. Shock & Denial - The unexpected has happened. "It is not possible"! "This cannot be happening to me!" "I must wake up from this bad dream".

The first reaction to learning about a terminal illness, loss, or death of a loved one is to deny the reality of the situation. It is a normal reaction to rationalize our overwhelming emotions. Denial is a common defense mechanism that buffers the immediate shock of the loss, numbing us to our emotions and reality.

2. Anger – Hurt, Pain – Too painful an experience! Rhetoric questions begin - "Why me?" "What have I done to deserve this?" "How could God have allowed this to happen to me?" "How am I supposed to cope with this?"

The pain of grief can also disrupt your physical health, making it difficult to sleep, eat, or even think straight. Such pain is psychosomatic, affecting your mind and body.

As reality sets in, you're faced with the pain of your loss. You may feel frustrated and helpless. These feelings later turn into anger. You might direct it toward other people, a higher power, or life in general. To be angry with a loved one who died and left you alone is natural, too.

3. Bargaining - Guilt & Fear – You are gripped with the fear of the known and unknown. You begging to think it is your fault. What has happened may not have happened if you…….. You start to believe there was something you could have done differently to safe your loved one. "I could have prevented this! " "If only we had sought medical attention sooner…If only we had tried to be a better person toward them… Ifl if! And If! "Had l known"

4. Depression - At this stage, you finally realize the true magnitude of your loss, and it depresses you. You may isolate yourself on purpose, reflect on things you did with your lost one, and focus on memories of the past. You may have feelings of emptiness or despair and wish you could do something to reverse the situation.

5. Acceptance & Healing In this final stage of grief, you accept the reality of your loss. IT HAS HAPPENED! It cannot be changed. Although you still feel sad, you're able to start moving forward with your life. "Well! So be it! I have to face it, life must continue! There is balm in Gilead to make the wounded whole

- Jer 8:22 – by the comfort of the Holy Spirit, there is a healing, a recovery and a hope in the Lord that through the love of God our Saviour all will be well.

Through the love of God our Saviour,

Through the love of God our Saviour, All will be well;
Free and changeless is His favour, All, all is well:
Precious is the blood that healed us;

Perfect is the grace that sealed us;
Strong the hand stretched forth to shield us;
All must be well.

Though we pass through tribulation, All will be well;
Christ hath purchased full salvation, All, all is well:
Happy still in God confiding;
Fruitful, if in Christ abiding;

Holy, through the Spirit's guiding;
    All must be well

We expect a bright tomorrow; All will be well;
Faith can sing through days of sorrow, All, all is well:
On our Father's love relying,
Jesus every need supplying,
Then in living or in dying,
All must be well. Amen.

QUESTION 100
WILL THERE BE A MARRIAGE IN HEAVEN?

Sing this chorus if you know it:-

When we get to heaven, at the Marriage Supper

All the saints shall gather, at the last assembly

No more heart breaking, No more sad parting,

Farewell to sorrow, Victory at last!

It is written, "Let us be glad and rejoice and give Him glory,

for the marriage of the Lamb has come, and His wife has made herself ready."

And to her it was granted to be arrayed in fine linen,

clean and bright, for the fine linen is the righteous acts of the saints.

Then he said to me, "Write: 'Blessed are those who are called to the marriage supper of the Lamb!' " And he said to me,

"These are the true sayings of God." Rev 19: 7 – 9.

Many bereaved people look forward to spending eternity with their spouse in heaven, especially if separated untimely by untimely death in their marriage. Earthly marriage is a sample of what is yet to come in heaven – the Marriage Supper of the Lamb. Try and make it to heaven, you will see your loved ones who have gone before you. Marriage between men and women ends at their death. So, there is no marriage in heaven between husband and wife again. Of course, Revelation chapter 19 describes the marriage of the bride of Christ with the Lord. The Scriptures teach that the Christian church is the bride of Christ.

A marriage ceremony is described in Revelation 19: 7 -9. The "bride" is made up of all believers in Jesus Christ. The "groom" is none other than Jesus Christ Himself. Jesus called Himself the bridegroom of Christians - Mathew 9:15. Christians are married to God and Christ under the terms of the New Testament covenant, as Israel was married to God under the terms of the Old Testament covenant. In passages like Ephesians 4:12 -16, 5: 25 -33, Apostle Paul used the marriage relationship of men and women to illustrate and teach the relationship of Christ to His church, proving that Christians are now married to Christ. It is also very clear that Christ and His bride are going to have the final marriage festivities, after His second coming, when the church would have been raptured.

We know we are in the last days of the latter times. We as Christians are waiting, looking forward to the Rapture. What John's vision in Revelation pictures is the wedding feast of the Lamb - Jesus Christ and His bride - the Church in its third phase. The implication is that the first two phases have already taken place. The first phase was completed on earth when each individual believer placed his or her faith in Christ as Savior. The dowry paid to the bridegroom's parent - God the Father is be the blood of Christ shed on the Bride's behalf on the Cross of Calvary. The Church on earth today, then, is "betrothed" to Christ, and, like the wise virgins in the parable, all believers should be watching and waiting for the appearance of the Bridegroom at the rapture.

The second phase symbolizes the rapture of the Church, when Christ comes to claim His bride and take her to the Father's house. The marriage supper then follows as the third and final step. It is our view that the marriage supper of the Lamb takes place in heaven between the rapture and the second coming (during the tribulation on earth). The marriage supper of the Lamb will take place after the Church has been taken to Heaven in the Rapture and following the judgment seat of Christ, but it will happen before we return with Christ to earth at His glorious appearing.

The participants of this incredible end time event will include the groom who is the Lamb – Jesus Christ and the bride who is the church. Every person who is a member of the body of Christ will be there as the bride. As a believer you are cordially invited to the "Marriage Supper of the Lamb". The moment you accepted Christ as your Lord and Savior you became part of His Bride to be. This will be your wedding feast. Have you accepted Jesus as your Lord and Saviour? You need to.

CONCLUSION

Let us hear the conclusion of the whole matter: Fear God and keep His commandments, for this is man's all duty. For God will bring every work into judgment, including every secret thing, whether good or evil. Ecclesiastes 12:13 -14.

"Hebrew 9:27 "And as it is appointed unto men once to die, but after this the judgment.""

There is life after death my dear reader. Where will you spend eternity? My friend, you need to be saved. I will conclude this piece of writing with the ABC of salvation. I pray you, if you have not accepted Jesus as your Lord and Saviour, do so right now. Going to heaven is as simple as ABC.

A - All have sinned and come short of the glory of God – Romans 3:23

The wages of sin is death – Romans 6:23, everlasting sorrow in Hell, No sin is allowed in heaven.

We must Admit we are sinners and in need of Jesus Christ

- We have to Accept Jesus as our Lord and personal Saviour

B. Believe that Jesus died on the cross for your sin, and rose again for your justification

- "For God so loved the world that He gave His only begotten Son, that whoever believes in Him should not perish but have everlasting life." John 3:16.

"But God demonstrates His own love for us, in that while we were still sinners, Christ died for us." Romans 5:8

C. If we CONFESS our sins, he is faithful and just to forgive us our sins, and to cleanse us from all unrighteousness. I John 1:9.

CHOOSE to trust Jesus alone for the forgiveness of your sins.

"That if thou shalt confess with thy mouth the Lord Jesus, and shalt believe in thine heart that God hath raised him from the dead, thou shalt be saved" Romans 10:9.

"For whosoever shall call upon the name of the Lord shall be saved". Romans 10:13.

We need to remember we all sin but the greatest gift of all God had his son Jesus Christ die for our sins. We ought to believe that Christ died for our sins. We must also confess and ask forgiveness of our sins. Jesus Christ is the only way to get to our Father up in Heaven.

Neither is there salvation in any other: for there is none other name under heaven given among men, whereby we must be saved. Acts 4: 12.

Have you asked Jesus to be your Savior? He's waiting to hear from you!

When you trust in Jesus Christ alone to save you, God forgives you! You become His child, and He promises you a home in heaven forever! Put your trust in Jesus as your Savior from sin. Do it today, and begin following Him by obeying His Word, the Bible.

Come to the Saviour, make no delay,

Here in his Word He's shown us the way

Here in our midst He's standing today,

Tenderly saying come

Refrain:

Joyful, joyful will the meeting be,

When from sin our hearts are pure and free

And we shall gather, Saviour to thee,

In our eternal home. Amen.

Pray this prayer - Dear Lord Jesus, Thank you for dying on the cross for my sin. Please forgive me. Come into my life. I receive You as my Lord and Savior. Now, help me to live for you the rest of this life. In the name of Jesus, I pray. Amen.

WELCOME TO THE FAMILY OF GOD! -If you have just prayed this prayer, you are welcome to the family of God. God is now your Father, Jesus is your Saviour and the Holy Spirit is now your guide. You are born again. Your name is written in the Book of Life. In case you have not been part of any church before, look for a Bible believing and holiness preaching Church like the Redeemed Christian Church of God to attend. This will enable you grow in the grace and in the knowledge of the Lord Jesus Christ. Congratulations! Wishing you a successful, Victorious Christian life in the name of Jesus. Amen.

Finally my brethren,

"… I commit you to God, and to the word of his grace, which is able to build you up, and to give you an inheritance among all them which are sanctified."

Acts 20:32.

"Now unto him that is able to keep you from falling, and to present you faultless before the presence of his glory with exceeding joy. To the only wise God our Saviour, be glory and majesty, dominion and power, both now and ever. Amen." Jude 24-25.

CONTACT

____

The writer – Pastor Dr. Mrs. Cecilia Gbemisola Obisakin is a Biblical Counselor most especially on family matters.

She is a Licensed Clinical Pastoral Counselor by the National Christian Counselors Association of the United States of America – NO.15397.

She is available for teaching, preaching, counseling, seminars, and workshops on Family matters.

You may call on +23450967220 – Nigeria

+2296868333 – Benin Republic or

 Email-   cgobisakin@hotmail.com.
Cslrcecilia60@gmail.com

We are trained to serve. We are at your service.

Shalom.

BIBLIOGRAHY

Finis, Jennings Dake. Dake's Annotated Reference Bible Old & New Testaments with Notes, Concordance and Index. Lawrenceville, Georgia, Dake Publishing, Inc. 2005.

Adams, Jay E. Marriage, Divorce and Remarriage in the Bible. Grand Rapids, Michigan: Zondervan Publishing House, 1980

Wheat, Ed. How to Save Your Marriage Alone. Grand Rapids, Michigan, Zondervan Publishing House, 1983.

Dag, Heward – Mills. Model Marriage – A Marriage Counseling Handbook. Hosanna Christian Bookshop & Publishing House, Benin City, Nigeria 2011.

Jim, Newheiser. Marriage Divorce and Remarriage. Critical Questions and Answers. Phillipsburg. PR Publishing 2017.

Elisabeth Kubler Ross and David Kessler. Understanding the Seven Stages of Grief. https://www.google.com/search.

Obisakin, Cecilia Gbemisola. Understanding Biblical Counseling – A Teaching and Counseling Manual on Christian Counseling, Marriage and family relationship. Triumph Publishing Bronx, New York. 2010.

Declaration – sample of complete wedding program –

(Order of Marriage Service in the Redeemed Christian Church of God) .www.rccg.org

Wikipedia is a multilingual online encyclopedia.

Obisakin, Cecilia Gbemisola. Premarital Counseling Made Simple – Somerest Ventures, Ikeja, Lagos. 2020.

ABOUT THE AUTHOR

Her Excellency, Pastor, Dr. Mrs. Cecilia Gbemisola Obisakin is a very resourceful, versatile, innovative and visionary woman of God. She is a full Pastor in the Redeemed Christian Church of God. She is currently serving with her husband – Pastor, Ambassador Lawrence Olufemi Obisakin; as wife of the Provincial Pastor – RCCG Benin Republic Province 1, Cotonou, Republic of Benin. She is a "Born teacher" by profession, and an Internationally Licensed Professional, Clinical, Pastoral Counselor by The National Christian Counselors

Association- NCCA, United States of America. She has a great, indefatigable passion for teaching, preaching, imparting Bible knowledge and encouraging applied principles of the Holy Scriptures.

Pastor Dr. Mrs. Cecilia Obisakin is a seasoned educationist and Christian counselor per excellence. She is the proprietress and first principal of Babcecil Schools, New Karu, Nasarawa state of Nigeria, founded 1996. A prolific writer, most of her Christian Literature are centered on Marriage Counseling or Family Life Education. She is national, an international and interdenominational preacher, teacher, speaker and seminarian on The Christian Marriage, Biblical Counseling, and Family affairs. She owns a Combined Bachelors of Arts degree in English Education – Unife (Now OAU) Ile-Ife, Nigeria - 1982; Post Graduate Diploma in Theology – RCBC Abuja chapter, 1997; Master degree in Biblical Counseling – Trinity College of the Bible and Seminary, Newburg, Indiana, USA 2010, and first Ph.D. 2014. She obtained a second Ph.D. in Christian Education from Andersonville Theological Seminary, Camilla Georgia USA -2017. She has been married for almost four decades, and she is blessed with children and grandchildren.

ABOUT THIS BOOK

The Bible says "Ask and it shall be given you, seek, and ye shall find, knock, and it shall be opened unto you" Mathew 7:7. For all those questions that have been asked in counseling sessions; in churches when preaching and teaching on "Family Forum"; in seminars and workshops on Marriage and family affairs - at home in Nigeria and abroad in America, Brazil, Canada, Europe, Israel and Switzerland; this book is the Answer.

The questions were generated from real life experiences, the concerns, interrogations from and discussion with Counselees. As an international marriage counselor of over thirty years, my counselees cut across different nations, race, status and age, but we offer only biblical advice to them in accordance with the Word of God.

Take time to read this book and pass it on to others. This book may be used as a wedding gifts for newlyweds. God will surely use it to encourage, inform, reform, correct and reestablish innumerous members of the family in the name of Jesus. Amen.